To Paris —

With Love

A Personal Odyssey

By Eric H Willis

Order this book online at www.trafford.com
or email orders@trafford.com

Most Trafford titles are also available at major online book retailers.

Printed in Victoria, BC, Canada.

ISBN: 978-1-4269-2166-7 (soft)
ISBN: 978-1-4269-2167-4 (hard)

Library of Congress Control Number: 2009940712

*Our mission is to efficiently provide the world's finest, most comprehensive book publishing
service, enabling every author to experience success. To find out how to publish your book, your
way, and have it available worldwide, visit us online at www.trafford.com*

Trafford rev. 11/5/2009

 www.trafford.com

North America & international
toll-free: 1 888 232 4444 (USA & Canada)
phone: 250 383 6864 ◆ fax: 812 355 4082

To Helga Louise

without whose inspiration

the first word could never

have been attempted

and

the last word never written!

Table of Contents

Foreword

Sometimes life deals some strange cards in marriage: death, sickness, deceit or just plain incompatibility. In mid life, the accumulated burden of any of these afflictions can be so stultifying, even devastating, as to seemingly foreclose any chance of happier days in the future. What follows is the story of a personal odyssey of two people, both of whom had been struggling to get from under their respective clouds, and were fortunate enough to have as the environment for their recovery -- Paris, France. I had been given leave of absence from the Office of Technology Assessment, US Congress, to be Director of Research of the International Energy Agency. Helga was still Assistant Executive Director of the Federal Communications Commission. Building a close relationship by Trans Atlantic telephone was not felt to be a viable option, so with a lot of courage Helga gave up her career to join me in Paris after I had established a beachhead there for eight months. It was also our fervent hope and prayer that if we succeeded in fashioning our own union it would create a stable background of encouragement and support for our children who, while nearly adult, were still in their formative years and who, for one reason or another, had not received a full measure of two parent support in recent years.

This narrative is written from the perspective of nearly thirty happy years later, and it is our hope that it will provide, with a bit of humor, a word picture for the benefit of our family and others of what it was like for us to "set up shop" in Paris, and to create a new life for ourselves. We will be for ever grateful to the many who were so ready to give their encouragement and support. We give thanks each day for our bounty, and our experience calls to mind the striving embodied in that saying of Robert Browning:

"Ah, but a man's reach should exceed his grasp,

Or what's a heaven for?"

Eric and Helga

Part One – A Beachhead in Paris: the first eight months

"La Vie Commence Demain"

1. Arriving in the City of Light

The airport bus was jam-packed as it left the gray round hulk of Roissy, Charles de Gaulle. The terminal we were leaving epitomized France's unyielding attempt to be different from other, and by inference, less imaginative countries. Spectacularly innovative, even exciting, in every respect except that it left no room whatever for future expansion. This key omission eventually led to a new terminal being built which proved indistinguishable from all the other airports the first terminal had studiously striven to avoid. But on that Sunday in May nineteen eighty, the terminal had a very special air about it – I had arrived with a one way ticket. The inescapable truth was that I was not making a return trip any time soon. Those return trips always had the warmth of knowing that you were going home; you bought your gifts, your duty free, and your boarding pass and the bold IAD on it assured you that at the end of a long day ahead you would be sleeping in your own bed. One could even tolerate the Immigration and Customs officials at Washington Dulles when they exuded their synthetic welcome. The otherwise long and uncomfortable taxi drive home would temporarily overcome the fatigue that drains both body and soul of everything but a overriding desire to curl up on the back seat and go to sleep. Such contemplation today was but a pipe dream – Paris was going to be home for the next five years.

Fellow passengers on an airport bus have a common anonymity, but for those forty minutes they are your only connection with the outside world. Where were they going ? Some were dozing – obviously they were coming home. Some looked terrified, some merely curious; some seemed bored, some wide eyed. *Les etrangers* gave themselves away by gazing fascinated as the white edifice *Sacre Coeur* appeared proudly on the *Bute de Montmatre* – this was indeed Paris. Even the Peripherique on that day held a fascination for me that I must confess it never held again, for it has all the charisma of an open sewer choked with vehicles and perfumed by their exhaust. The bus disgorged its human load at *Port Maillot*, and I hailed a taxi from the rank. In what must have been excruciating french, I instructed the somewhat graceless driver to take me to my hotel in *Passy*. *Passy* used to be a separate village on the outskirts of Paris, but is now incorporated within the city limits. It maintains its old village road layout, and the narrow streets give it a certain charm. It is bounded on one side by the *Bois de Bologne* and on the other by its former twin village of *Auteil*. It was just my luck on this Sunday afternoon that my taxi entered the Rue de Passy just as the lead runners of the Paris Marathon started to cross it. The normally frenetic Parisian driver was perfectly at ease having a grandstand view of the ensuing procession, for you would be surprised at the wonders it was doing to the taxi meter with no effort at all on his part. I took this to be something of an omen.

Passy is also the home of the Organization for Economic Cooperation and Development (OECD), known a little unkindly as the rich nations Club. It is housed in the delightful Chateau de la Muette, an old but elegant hunting lodge near the Bois de Bologne. Work is mostly carried on in more prosaic but pleasant buildings nearby. An integral part of the OECD is the International Energy Agency, the IEA, which was created in 1974 to coordinate the Western Nations response to the Arab Oil Embargo of 1973. Since the push for its creation came heavily from the Americans, it was seen by the French as merely a ploy by the United States to control the sharing of scarce oil resources around the globe, and an irate French Foreign Minister, Michel Jobert, had refused to join. As part of the inducement to join, the United States had offered to share its extensive energy technology research, in which it was then investing heavily, with the other nations of the OECD towards the common good. The other twenty one nations did in fact join the IEA, to some extent because of this not inconsequential inducement. With the notable exception of France it was set up as part of the OECD under the leadership of a very able German economist named Ulf Lantzke. Thus the curious situation had arisen of having the IEA head quartered in the capital of a country which was not a member. To some, who might be considered only slightly cynical, this did not constitute an unmitigated disaster. The Energy Research Office was a flourishing part of the IEA with about fifty active joint international projects in place, and I was arriving in Paris this Sunday to assume its Directorship the following morning.

The marathon runners went on their weary way, and the traffic resumed its course oblivious to the stragglers who were now irrelevant to the outcome of the race. I checked in at the Hotel Gavarni which modestly but correctly announces itself as *"Un hôtel agreéable dans le calme de Passy"*. It was run by an amiable couple who had, it turns out, just taken over and who would turn out to be very good friends years later. It was in a side street off the Rue de Passy in one of those old town houses that lent themselves to conversion to two star hotels with diminutive rooms, and the later additions of even more diminutive bathrooms. But it was clean, the people were friendly and spoke good English, and the price was right. For the moment, then, it was a convenient launching pad for a new life ahead.

I had changed jobs quite a few times before, sometimes entailing changed cities and even countries. Thus there was nothing particularly novel in my going through this routine once again. But this time it was to be different – very different ! To begin with, I was living in the environment of a foreign language. To be sure I had emigrated to the United States from Britain where it was alleged that the language was the same, but although that contention could be challenged, it did not pose insuperable difficulties. It is also true that I had learned French from the age of seven to the age of fourteen, and normal folk with that level of education might be expected to have a reasonable working knowledge of conversational French. Alas, I have an unfortunate tone deaf ear which renders me incapable of detecting the nuances of either music or spoken French. So that although I had a passable comprehension of the written word it did not extend to the minimum requirements for purchasing a few elementary items in the hardware store. Strangely, I was foolishly confident that I could overcome this minor impediment to day to day living, and treasured the illusion that the purchase of a television set would rectify all ills.

No, the principal difference this time was that I ws sitting here in the hotel room having burned some significant bridges, and had only just made a fleeting start to buiding alternative ones. The feeling of being alone was pervasive – everything in my life at that moment was new, and some crucial reference points, so necessary for an orderly life, were missing. Most notably were the absence of friends, home , job, colleagues, car, family, and most importantly a spouse. The latter was no small matter, for I had in my pocket a very significant document – a Legal Separation Agreement freshly signed on the way to Dulles Airport as I left the United States. My marriage was over in every practical sense, if not from the final legal standpoint. This Agreement had thus allowed me to arrive in Paris unfettered and alone, as I had wished. Nevertheless there was a residual element of sadness. I had long adhered to the notion, almost as an article of faith, that marriage is an honorable estate not lightly to be cast aside. I am even more of this conviction thirty years later..

A serious resolve on my part to terminate an unhappy state of affairs been on my mind since Christmas; how to bring this resolve to a satisfactory conclusion was by no means clear. Then, quite out of the blue two unforseen events happened which showed the way.

The first was a phone call from my friend Jack Vanderryn saying that the job of Director of Research for the International Energy Agency in Paris was becoming vacant, and the Department of Energy would very much like to put my name forward. This invitation was an honor in itself; not only was this a prestigious position but the prospect of spending a few years in Paris was not to be sniffed at in any circumstance. This opportunity not only provided a splendid opportunity, but also provided a bone fide scenario for the break-up which had only been fuzzy before.

The second unforseen and equally happy occurrence was the advent of Helga into my life in mid March; this changed the dynamics of the situation completely. How this happened is Helga's story, and you must ask her sometime about it when she is in an expansive mood. Suffice to say that whereas prior to this there existed a very definite "push" factor to end the marriage, now there was an unequivocal "pull". The "pull" had established a goal; something to be worked for rather than against.

My son Nigel, then twenty-two, had traveled over with me as far as England and was currently staying with my Mother. He was poised to join me to set up shop in these new surroundings, and I looked forward to his coming immensely — for all his young years, he was to be a tower of strength. The fleeting sadness of the moment was more than offset by the prospect of a new dawn, of which the first rays of light had appeared over the horizon but not enough to see clearly the way ahead. This story, would lose much of its meaning if it lost sight of the bringing of this "way ahead" to its bountiful fruition; without wishing to be overly sentimental, it is a continuing Love Story still in progress twenty two years later. The loneliness of that first evening in Paris turned out to be but the prelude to a new beginning. The stage would be set in Paris, but both unexpectedly and providentially Helga, of whom much more later, had already become the star of the play which was about to unfold.

In a thoughtful and welcoming gesture, Leslie Boxer soon to be my Deputy, and his daughter Sylvie, took me out for a Chinese Dinner in the evening, and I was thankful to get away from the inevitable introspection of the newcomer for a while. Returning to the Hotel, I turned in for what transpired to be a fitful night's sleep, wondering what impressions the morning would bring.

"La Vie Commence Demain"

2. First day at School.......... the "New Boy".

As an American, schooled in being punctual and appearing eager to justify one's existence, I left the hotel at eight the next morning to meet my new colleagues and embark upon this challenging job in the international arena. I immediately had an odd awareness that I was the only person on the street: save for one furtive individual, craving anonymity by looking the other way as his dog relieved itself on the side walk. Other than that, the only moving thing in sight was a rather decrepit delivery van that made its desultory way passed me. I checked my watch against a clock on a bank to make sure I had adjusted it to allow for the time change; there was no mistake. I arrived at the OECD just as the door was opening, and was met by a blank stare from the *huissier,* or usher, who informed me that no one was yet in the agency, let alone my new office. It appeared that nine o'clock was the first civilized hour to be seen in a Parisian office. Despite their cultivated threatening exterior, *huissiers* turned out to be either a mine of information or a mountain of obstruction, depending on which way you were to rub them. The huissiers at the IEA were no exception, and bent rules and interpreted regulations in the most imaginative ways with the magic phrase "*on s'arrange*". The IEA was housed in a new part of the OECD on the Rue de Franqueville, which had elegant mahogany paneling, doors and closets. The Agency also had a much older part clearly built in times of more stringent budgets. Predictably, I was ushered into a rather forbidding and somewhat shabby room with a scuffed floor and a grubby rug which did not at all conform to my ideas of a gleaming international organization. This was to be home from home for the next five very happy years.

The secretary was next to arrive, late of course. She showed her flustered embarrassment not at being late, which was tacitly assumed, but at finding the new boss sitting at his desk with demonstrably nothing much to do on his first morning. Actually, she was not really my secretary, for the permanent one was naturally on maternity leave waiting to go on post maternity leave, and on returning immediately to take the vacation time she had accrued on both. When she did at last return, it was the turn of the temporary secretary to be pregnant. When a third secretary became pregnant in her turn, the uninitiated might have been tempted to look for a causal relationship between the chair they sat on in the outer office and their subsequent condition. This was my first introduction to the French labor laws under which the OECD operated. As a rule of thumb, since one secretary was always pregnant at any one time one needed twice the number of staff on the pay roll to fill the slot of each person actually working. It was a profound revelation to us all that, in France, pregnancies take twelve rather than the more conventional nine months.

Indoctrination is normally accorded the new boy on his first morning, and I was no exception. I was taken over to the Chateau by a delightful young woman called Elfie, who is a good friend to this day. The Chateau is where the administration of the OECD took place – depending upon one's rank, one either worked in a former ballroom with chandeliers or a bare garret flanked by a sloping roof. People who were to help the newcomer lived in garrets, and the doorway was the only place one could stand upright. They attempted to explain, with mixed success, the mysteries of the french social security system, the payroll deductions and, although the OECD was then less than twenty five years old, its byzantine structure of salaries and allowances. Somewhat to my surprise, I was told that I was one of only a dozen or so mucky-mucks who were accorded special deference by virtue of their exalted rank. This status did not last long. I soon realized that although great globs of francs would be coming in to my bank account, great globs would also be going out, so that an imposing salary on paper was not about to translate into any high living. My salary was to be tax free which, true to form, the US Government would not accept. The French ingeniously got around this minor problem by reimbursing the amount of the tax I had to pay. Since I would have to pay tax on the reimbursement, this charade went on ad infinitum. Nevertheless, finding oneself to be a mucky-muck required immediate and appropriate action, so I hastened to open an account with a mucky-muck bank, the Banque Rothschild, whose checks were never questioned nor ID ever required. Just don't bounce one!

Where to live? To answer this question, the Chateau had a housing bureau run my a somewhat gaunt but attractive woman who, in common with many french women of a certain seniority, continued to exuded natural sexual charm as a matter of course. Five years later it was no different, and even the later news that Helga was in the wings had a barely perceptible dampening effect. Apart from finding some interesting prospects of possible accommodation at exorbitant prices, I chalked up the encounter with the OECD help as enlightened education which one could but treasure. If this was France, whew !

I next interviewed the members of my staff; it was multinational. There was always an American and a Japanese on the staff because between them those countries provided nearly fifty per cent of the IEA budget. A German, a Dutchman, and an Australian made up the remainder, together with my Deputy, Leslie Boxer, who was an Englishman very experienced in the conduct of international energy affairs. It is a testimony to the working relationships that we developed that three of these persons remain very close friends twenty years later. My predecessor, Milton Klein, had also been an American and I was much indebted to him for the broad foundation that he had laid down. There was a scientific oversight Committee for Research and Development drawn from the twenty-one member nations, and it was a pleasant surprise to find that my old friend Donald Kerr was its Chairman, and happily remained so throughout my tenure. Today he is a neighbor, and with his wife Allison, the closest of friends.

Taken altogether, it seemed a propitious moment to be taking over the reigns that day, but later with the change of Administration in Washington at the end of that year one was to be reminded once again how quickly political winds can shift. So with my head spinning I adjourned to the nearest bistro for a tankard of beer, beef steak, and pommes frittes. It was Maytime, and the horse chestnuts were still blooming along the nearby *Jardins de Ranelagh*. The gardens prominently displayed a dramatic statue of the French story teller, *La Fontaine*, and at his feet the fox and the crow from one of his stories . To complete the appeal to the child in one, a functioning children's carousel and a Punch and Judy Show completed one of those scenes which endears Paris to the soul forever. It was a moment for relaxation, and to say, "Perhaps this might be just alright---even for five years"

3. Where to call home?.

The first few weeks always seem like an eternity on any new job, and compounded by the unfamiliar surroundings this was no exception. It was with some sense of anticipation therefore that I went to meet Nigel two weeks later at Roissy Charles de Gaulle. We stayed the first night or two together at the Gavarni. Clearly, two of us in that small room was not a viable option for even a short term , let alone the prospect of paying interminable hotel room prices. I had been asking around, and had come up with a place at No. 5 *Rue de Franqueville*, just a block or so from the OECD. It was graced with the name of *Hôtel de Cigognes,* which is french for a "Stork" – it had little in common with either a hotel or a stork. Our "flat" consisted of a double bed with a cot at its foot. There was a bathroom next door, which was also passed off as our kitchen with the inclusion of some rudimentary museum pieces of a doubtful vintage. Never mind, we could prepare some of our own meals. We duly moved in, and started to become Parisians.

The accommodation was on the first floor overlooking the normally sleepy street and, since this was by far the hottest part of the fairly dismal summer of 1980, the windows were constantly open. At night time the scene changed dramatically; part of downtown Casablanca had seemingly been transferred to Paris in its entirety, complete with vibrant voices and unrestrained traffic. Taxis would pull up in the wee hours of the morning to disgorge inebriated passengers whose voices would do justice to any Imam on a minaret at daybreak during

Ramadan, an experience forever ingrained in my mind. The ensuing din and the idling diesel engines would thump their way into your consciousness through any sleep you may have had. This provided us with a key lesson in house hunting; never, ever, get an apartment facing the street that is not at least five stories up, for the "canyon" effect has always to be taken into account.

Meanwhile, I was thrashing around for somewhere worthy of calling "home". I saw some desperate places. One candidate was on the Isle Saint Louis, near my colleague Niels de Terra, overlooking the Seine under the shadow of the flying buttresses of Notre Dame. The location was as authentically Parisian as one could get, but the facilities had not changed much since Louis XIV was a lad. Our housing assistance ladies in the Chateau had come up with a few addresses, but most were straight out of La Bohéme. Real estate agencies proved a disaster. One would have absolutely no Germans, which given Helga's antecedents was a non starter; another wanted me to buy his gold plated swan necked bath tub faucets at a price equivalent to six months salary. Eventually, we were given the address of 37 Boulevard Murat, in what we later affectionately came to call " the low rent district" of the otherwise very fashionable 16th Arrondissment.

The apartment building had been built at the height of the "New Brutalist de Gaulle Concrete Chic" in 1964, and the apartment itself was termed a "duplex. That meant that it occupied two floors, the 10th and the 11th, joined by an intriguing rounded marble staircase. It was decorated, if that be the term, in a hideous cross between speed psychedelic and nouvelle victoriana. The wall paper was offensive beyond belief, and it would be one of the first things to go. The floor was covered with a grey carpeting called moquette laid over bare concrete; the grayness was partly original but mostly from the accrued grime of the previous twenty years. Light fixtures were left to your imagination, since the only clue to their possible location were two bare wires protruding from gaping holes in the wall. The front door was apparently declared surplus from the Maginot Line, for its intricate lock system and sliding bars were designed to keep out a tank. The kitchen was a short corridor which could hold two people at the same time only if one of them were to breath in. Something resembling a gas stove was cunningly disguised by a heavy encrustation from years of burnt offerings whose removal defied even Nigel's persuasion with a chisel. The refrigerator would conceivably hold a loaf of french bread if stood on its end, but given the nature of the Parisian climate in winter the de facto refrigerator was obviously the window box outside the kitchen window. A washing machine of uncertain vintage was of a novel construction which gyrated in random fashion with a full load of a pair of undershorts and at least two pocket handkerchiefs. The sink would obviously prove functional if its connection to the sewer was ever restored by generous applications of draino. Other than that, everything was in perfect working order. To be honest, all this was a distinct improvement over all the other places I had seen prior to this which had featured nothing more than a bare earthenware kitchen sink in an otherwise barren landscape.

If one were really serious and ridiculously energetic, as in the delivery of a sofa or an armoire, one could climb the ten flights of stairs to the landing. Mercifully, there was an elevator which most of the time worked. It had no interior door, and even the dog was careful to keep away from the "moving wall". We discovered that a notice inscribed with the delphic words *"En Panne"* could be roughly translated as "The damn thing is broken, and may possibly be fixed some time next week if you are lucky". We found, later, that all was not entirely lost when this notice appeared - one merely took the next elevator bank up to the roof, walked across the roof to the next elevator bank, which was ours, and came down a couple of flights of stairs to our landing. Simple ! It was in this way my Mother was to find her way to the apartment in a wheel chair on one occasion assisted by a swarthy Moroccan of immense strength. The views were impressive, with the Eiffel Tower to the rear, and a view of St Cloud over the Bois de Bologne from a reasonably spacious terrace off the bedroom in the front.

Despite the obvious drawbacks, the location was excellent, with a straight shot up Boulevard Suchet to work at the OECD. The local quartier had much to commend it, with the old village center of Auteuil close at hand. In short, this was about as good as it was going to get, and we took it. Signing the lease had the air of participating in a mediaeval ritual. The landlord has to have been among the most miserable human beings I had ever met. Politically he was far to the right of de Gaulle, whom he vocally considered a traitor to the glory of France. Personally he was less than endearing with his disheveled appearance and clothes that had never seen the need for a wash tub never mind a dry cleaner . He lived not far away in Rue Chavez in a grotty apartment far inferior to the one he was leasing us. I signed my name on the appropriate"*Lu et Approuvé*" lines. Later it transpired that I had initialed a clause which confined any rent increases to the official published cost of living index increases. This legal index was fortunately the same one which was used to compute my housing allowance from the OECD, so for once I was abreast of the game. He proved to be very vocal, even angry, in his regret at my signing this clause, particularly since the law was clear that he could never evict me as long as I stuck to the terms of the lease. We sealed the deal with a toast in some quite inferior wine in marked contrast to the excellent Scotch he had imbibed when visiting us. In all, it could be fairly described as a dismal experience.

Having settled the problem of where the permanent address was to be, attention now had to be given to shipping the household goods to that address. Ulf Lantzke, my boss, graciously suggested it would be a good idea for me to go back to Washington "*en mission*" to personally supervise the moving crew -- I can only conclude that he must have had some bad moving experiences of his own along the way! I crossed my fingers and left Nigel at the *Cigognes* and headed back to Washington. After all, I told myself, at twenty two he was a big boy now and could take care of himself -- which he did, admirably.

Back once more in Washington, it proved to be one of the hottest summers on record, and my heart went out to the moving crew when they duly arrived to vacate the house for renters to move in.i had been through a transatlantic move of an entire household before, and had nourished the fond hope that it would have been for the last time. Coming from Cambridge, England, in 1964, the English movers had seemingly assembled all the household goods in one rectangular pile in a warehouse, and then to have constructed a container made of wooden planks <u>around</u> it. Shipping technology had markedly improved since that day, and now one used dedicated containers that go on ships like so many match boxes. Nevertheless it was a leap of faith to believe that this huge container in the road outside, being filled with crates and furniture, would miraculously turn up unscathed outside the apartment in Paris – but that it did, for there was not a single breakage. Then there was only the small matter of negotiating those ten flights of stairs with the larger pieces of furniture. But then of course, they were French movers in Paris, and were adept at getting large pieces through a seeming keyhole.

The Wessynton house had been rented, and it was time to get everything out for the incoming tenants. I was more than overjoyed to see Helga again, and stayed with her for a few glorious days. Helga and I had made an instant commitment to each other before my leaving in May, but intentions are one thing and cold hard logistics, particularly carried out transatlantic, are another. At some point, she would be coming to Paris, and so her interests figured heavily in plans from now on. She had remnants of the wallpaper which had been torn down, so she knew in just what condition we had first seen it. Nevertheless, she approved of the apartment in principle, and I only hoped that it would live up to its billing.

I was more than glad to escape from this scene of frenetic activity and seek refuge with Helga at the days end. We resolved that she would come over on vacation in August when I would be more settled. She was at that time Assistant Executive Director of the Federal Communications Commission, and could not get away at the drop of a hat, but it gave us both something to look forward to.

4. Settling in.

Thanks to the invaluable help of Leslie Boxer, who initiated me into to the time honored tradition of extracting discounts and mark downs, we set about ordering some of the necessities, such as bedding. We visited the emporium of *Au Bon Marché,* which its upper floors, at that time, resembled more of a glass covered arcade. The glass had sprung leaks, and the rain had dripped down upon the bedding department below. The resulting stains would take some clever explaining over the years, but the significant mark down plus the discount brought the price down from the stratospheric to the merely exorbitant. I bought it. It comprised two single Dunlopillo foam beds which locked together to form one queen sized bed, so that for the period Nigel would be with me we could each have a proper bed – something we were looking forward to after "camping out".

Accustomed as we were to American prices, we were experiencing the first of many sticker shocks, although admittedly the US Dollar was at its lowest ebb against the French Franc, at 3.96 to the dollar. Since I was paid in French Francs, nearly everything in France seemed expensive when translated into dollars. In later years the Dollar was to buy 10.60 French Francs, and things were not quite as rosy for us since significant obligations remained in the United States, pensions etc, and which were of course denominated in dollars.

Eric H. Willis

We were to take possession of the apartment on June 28th, so we arranged for the beds to be delivered the same day. I had to go to Zurich that week to speak at some anniversary being held by the Swiss Nuclear Energy Establishment near Winterthur. My speech was totally inappropriate for the occasion, which was more in keeping with a beer swilling "Oktoberfest" than a serious symposium. It was almost humiliating, and I said some rude words about my boss Ulf Lantzke for off loading this chore onto me. My embarrassment was increased by the presence of my immaculately dressed Mother-in-Law to be, Hertha Schmitz Mancy, who was visiting Zurich at the time, and who I had invited to the "event". In the evening I called for her at the St. Gottard Hotel, and we made up for the debacle to some extent by having a fine dinner together in the Altstadt of Zurich.

There were, however two redeeming features to the otherwise disappointing trip, which were as unexpected as they were welcome. The first was that I had the opportunity to have dinner with my friend John Evans and his family who lived beside the *Zurichsee*. Beside being a most pleasant evening, it transpired that the Evans's owned an apartment in *Mürren,* in the *Bernese Oberland* of Switzerland. He generously offered the use of the apartment for me to stay in. I accepted at once, for I thought that this might make a splendid vacation spot for Helga and I when she came over in August. The second redeeming feature was the not inconsiderable honorarium of 1000 Swiss Francs, which was immediately earmarked to pay for Helga's air fare on that trip!.

On my return to Paris, I caught the venerable PC bus to the new apartment; PC stands for *Petite Ceinture,* a small belt, and it wends its lugubrious way endlessly around the boundaries of Paris. The PC is a Paris institution, and is never called by its full name. I arrived just in time to find the Au Bon Marché men walking down the stairs having delivered the beds. My colleague Bernd Kramer had picked up sheets and blankets from Helga while on a visit to Washington, and had kindly brought the large bundle back to Paris for me. So as far as the bedding was concerned we could at least sleep comfortably.

Now we had to set about making the place habitable in preparation for the eventual arrival of the household goods from Washington. As I mentioned earlier, the wallpaper was quite awful, and redecorating was an urgent necessity. Our landlord surprisingly acquiesced in the desecration of his decor, which included the demolition of a closet which would increase the size of the living room significantly. Through our concierge, who turned out to be a mine of information about everything and everybody in the quartier, I secured the services of a janitor, Monsieur Luchere ,who ran one of the apartment buildings in Boulevard Suchet. He moonlighted, which somehow meant most of the day, as a painter and we set about removing all the offending wallpaper, and painting the walls a light cream. The transformation was startling---from grim drabness, light! The apartment had a small study off the living room, and a very presentable dining room. Upstairs there were three bedrooms and two bathrooms. To be exact, the second bathroom contained an antique collection of shower plumbing which had long ago given up the unequal struggle with corrosion, and was blocked solid. The Louvre didn't want it so it was torn out and replaced with something approaching modern fixtures; it proved an admirable addition. The main bathroom contained an enormous bathtub, and a wash basin the size they ought to be – big!

Visits to member countries of the IEA were part of the job, and another of Ulf Lantzke's off-loadings took me on a quick trip to Stockholm to give yet another speech – it was a case of showing the flag. Being close to midsummer's day, there was no perceptible darkness, and since the hotel provided no blinds, there was not a lot of sleep. A car called for me after breakfast, I was driven to the meeting hall, I duly gave my speech at the appointed time, and the same car promptly delivered me back to the Airport. I hope I gave good value, for I got precious little out of if except all work and no sleep. I was, however, able to get the return flight to Paris via Copenhagen so that I was able to visit my old friends Anita and Henrik Tauber for an enjoyable evening and overnight stay. Henrik had been a close collaborator from my research days in Cambridge. This absence from Paris of course meant leaving Nigel alone to the tender mercies of the City and in charge of our new home. He was already enrolled in the *Alliance Français* so that he might occupy his time reasonably pleasantly, and perhaps even learn some French. A side benefit was the opportunity to make some new and cosmopolitan friends. What better than to hold a spaghetti party in his new home, which he often advertised as a pent-house apartment. True in fact, but not what that term conjures up. The less I knew about this party, the less I wanted to know. It's success seemed assured with the quaffing of liberal quantities of wine, and since no ostensible damage was done and as there were no complaints, all's well that ends well.

Getting started in a very empty Paris apartment necessarily meant the acquisition of some tools. This is where some fundamental education began. In the normal course of events one takes the names of small household items for granted, but when one moves to a foreign country, one has to learn this knowledge all over again. The hardware store is the *bricollage*, a *vis* is a screw, and naturally a *tournevis* is a screw-driver, and on infinitum. My American drill was quite hopeless when it came to making holes in walls. In America, you can make a hole in a wall just by leaning on it, but here they were made of *beton*, concrete. One needs a percussion drill, and a high powered one at that.

Naturally, there was an immediate need for some essential household appliances. *Le Printemps* is a big department store in the *Boulevard Haussman*, and there we sought the television which was to be so useful in mastering French. This was an illusion soon to be shattered .The model which seemed best, and most affordable, was a Philips with about a fifteen inch screen. This "affordablity" turned out to be a relative term, for it cost just on a thousand dollars at prevailing exchange rates. Today, I can buy a forty-two inch flat panel set in America for just half that, not even taking inflation into account. While at *Le Printemps*, we took the opportunity to invest in a combined washer and drier, *lavage et secheur*. As I mentioned, one had been provided in the kitchen of the apartment, but it had proven unequal to the normally routine task of standing up to Nigel's attempts to operate it. The defunct cadaver had been consigned to our locker room in the basement, where it was resurrected five years later to be in its appointed place when we left. The model chosen was a Siemens, which gave one some confidence that it would be more robust to withstand

Nigel's ministrations. It had a number of program cycles, measured in hours, which were encrypted on little cards of no obvious value but nevertheless printed in five languages. They told you which knobs to twiddle for any desired outcome, but the end results were remarkably similar. It had a horizontally rotating drum made of stainless steel with a construction which would have made a panzer regiment proud. It would rotate with a very audible sloshing sound, and then stop and rest as if to ponder a while. It assumed one had no hot water available, so it employed a heater which eventually reached a temperature which qualified as hot; the drying cycle took a full hour to reach an acceptable level of dampness. The lapse time for a modest load was about three hours and, as a matter of record, this machine further reduced my bank account by another one thousand dollars.

About this time I managed to get a dose of the Paris Crud, which sent me to bed sweating up a storm. It was a relief to have Nigel to take care of me, for it was accompanied by a debilitating weakness. It was a nasty experience, and the occasion of my first brush with the french ritual of "visiting the Doctor". My secretary recommended a no nonsense woman doctor, Madame Fodor, who suited me, and later Helga, just fine and proved a reliable friend. She had her *cabinet* in an apartment in Passy. The scene was repeated many times over the years with others in the medical or dental professions. One invariably ascended a threadbare staircase wrapped around an elevator which was predictably *en panne* to a landing with imposing double doors. An elderly retainer, whose face exhibited no visible expression, took your name and ushered you into a salon. It was almost as if you were in an ante room awaiting to be shown into the presence of Louis XIV. It was ornate beyond description, in a faded way, with artefacts of a bygone era and uncomfortable period piece chairs. The high windows had drapes whose pattern had long since ceased to be recognizable, and the threadbare carpet had seen many feet across it in its time. Taken together, the surroundings left one with more of a feeling of foreboding than confidence.

Transportation was the next matter on the agenda; so far we had not ventured outside the City, and it would be great to start even some modest exploration. There was also a good, but vacant, parking spot in the basement of the building beckoning to be filled. The OECD had an arrangement with a company, Sodexa, which sold cars to diplomats. I was slowly getting used to the fact that although I did not feel a diplomat, there were times when that status presented distinct advantages. This was one such time. The sales tax on cars in France seemed to me prohibitive, which seemed to run counter to the profusion of spanking new cars on the streets of Paris. The salesman duly came to my office, and I placed an order for a Peugeot 505. I had seen and inspected this model in a showroom on the Champs Elysees when I was visiting Paris for the job interview in February, and it was impulse buying in its most virulent form – I just wanted THAT car. We settled on jade green, with an opening roof and tweed upholstery. It was one of the best buys I ever made. Nigel and I, accompanied by one of our IEA drivers, went to Sodexa to pick it up. Too bad the gas gage didn't work, but such trivia aside I ventured into the flow of Parisian traffic for the first time in my own car. We had wheels !

Nigel and I made a quick weekend trip to England to see the Formula One Grand Prix at Brands Hatch. I was hoping to take the new car to England for its first voyage, but since I still had temporary plates the French authorities would not allow the car abroad. So this time we traveled by plane, and brought my mother, Win, back with us. We also brought some small cabin trunks which we had temporarily left behind at Win's home until such time as we were settled. Nigel had taken a great liking to Branston Pickle, and had secreted a cache of jars for safety among the clothing in the trunks. The lid of each jar had popped open, probably from the pressurization in the plane, and the resulting mess was a joy to behold. The recently cleaned suits in Washington went straight away back to the dry cleaners in Paris! For some reason we never understood, it turned out that Parisian dry cleaners were three or four times as costly as those in Washington

Mother soon settled in with us with the very barest of furniture, and Nigel concocted some imaginative sleeping arrangements using some recently acquired patio furniture. There was a diminutive kitchen table which was at least something to put food on. The beauty of Paris living is that one can obtain the most mouth watering creations at the local *Charcuterie* and the *Plats de Jour*. Cooking is made very easy, and this made up, to a large extent, for our lack of domestic cuisine. The painter was soon hard at work redecorating and had nearly finished when, in mid-July, we looked down from the balcony one morning to see the container with our furniture parked in the street outside. What a celebration! Soon there was furniture in the Living Room, a dining table where a dining table ought to be, and rugs on the floor to hide at least some of the gray moquette. There were pots and pans to cook with, plates to eat off, and knives and forks in place of fingers. Mother could now make pots of tea to her heart's content, and we felt that something approaching a home was starting to emerge after all the urban camping of the previous two months.

Nigel and I both had a common interest in the mail box. Nigel was expecting letters from his girl-friend Lori, now his wife and the mother of three of our wonderful grandchildren. I was likewise anticipating letters from Helga, now also my wife of nearly thirty years. One or the other of us was disappointed on occasion when the other read his letter with barely concealed smugness. With Mother Win still with us, and Nigel's stay in Paris coming to its end, we decided on a trip out of Paris in the new car. Win, by then eighty, was a comforting presence in any situation with her irrepressible wit, and she was a joy to have with us. We made our way to the Loire Valley, and stayed overnight at Blois. One of the Chateaux we visited was Amboise, which stands on a bluff above the River Loire. It was raining a bit, so Nigel and I left Win in the car. We intended to take a tour, but there was a slight delay before it started. We sheltered from the rain in a waiting room which had been formerly a very small chapel built into the high chateau wall. As Nigel happened to glance down, he was astonished to see inscribed in the stone wall a legend which read:

"Here lie the Mortal Remains of Leonardo da Vinci"

I could not believe that we had almost literally stumbled over the tomb of this genius. Later I found there was a famous painting depicting Leonardo dying in the arm of François Premier at Amboise. Who could not fall in love with that region with one magnificent chateau after another, and I took the opportunity to reserve a room at the Auberge St Michelle at Chambord for when Helga would arrive in August.

Eventually, I had to say goodbye to both Nigel and Win at Charles de Gaulle Airport. I would certainly miss Nigel who had been such a strength since his arrival. It was with a feeling of some sadness then that I drove back to Boulevard Murat to assume bachelor status for the next six months. At least I was on an even keel, and could turn my attention to IEA matters, and the fascinating activities that were already beginning to consume me

5.   IEA .....responding to the Arab Oil Embargo

After the interval of thirty years, it is difficult to recreate, let alone rationalize, the impact of the Arab oil embargo of 1973 following the Arab-Israeli War of that year. It is worthwhile recounting, briefly, the gravity of the situation as it was then perceived for it impacted daily life in an all pervasive way, and the economic consequences would threaten to bring the Industrial World to its knees. It is hard to overemphasize the situation facing governments of the Industrialized World, because the potential damage was catastrophic enough to elicit a vigorous political response to keep their economies afloat. It was the consequent political pressure among member countries of the OECD that was instrumental in creating the International Energy Agency to share oil supplies equitably, and at the same time address the perceived need for cooperation in international energy technology research..

Casting ones mind back to the period, it was perhaps the sight of lines of cars stretching around city blocks in order to get a few gallons of gasolene that remain so vivid, and they were.. a powerful incentive for politicians to "do something". Gas prices rose by factors of three or four in a very short time, which quickly affected the economy before any countermeasures could be put in place. Any politician who might have expressed even a modicum of caution over how to proceed would never have survived his next electi7on. Voices of the free market, if there were any, were mute and voices of all political complexions clamored for government action. The problem was immediate, demonstrable, and urgent. Inflation, interest rates and unemployment rose dramatically with the result that the growth in the Gross Domestic Product actually went negative in 1974 and, coupled with Watergate, directly affected the Presidential Election of 1976. It was an economic disaster of serious dimensions with no apparent end in sight. Compounding this picture, caused by the embargo alone, was the then long term outlook for both oil and natural gas supplies. The outlook for gas by the year 2000 was particularly gloomy: domestic reserves looked like being severely restricted. For oil, it was not so much the amount of the reserves, it was where they were located. Since the bulk of the reserves were, and still are, in the Middle East, the industrialized world was open to serious political and economic blackmail: the economies had to break their over-dependence on OPEC oil, particularly that from Middle East sources.

The Iranian revolution and the hostage taking at the American Embassy in Teheran in 1978, with the embargo still in place, gave rise to a second hike in the oil price, this time towards $40 per barrel. This led to the GDP growth going negative for the second time in the decade, with a big spike in the level of inflation. The term "stagflation" came into vogue to describe the phenomenon of high inflation coupled with stagnation in the economy as a whole. As did President Ford before him, President Carter was to forfeit reelection for a second term in 1980, partly as a result.

In 1974, natural gas reserves in the US were thought to have peaked and were starting to decline. Washington Gas Co. in the Capital area, curtailed the use of natural gas as a heating source in new housing developments, advocating instead the installation of electric driven heat pumps. When I was in the Energy Research and Demonstration Agency, ERDA, in 1977, with natural gas then below $2 per million BTU, we published a report on natural gas which drew the conclusion that if the price were right we would have domestic natural gas coming out of our ears. This later proved to be the case, but in the meantime we were cruelly ridiculed in the press. The Wall Street Journal gave us a particularly hard time in an editorial entitled "ERDAgate" (A parody on Watergate) Predictions like ours, which dared to say that there would be plenty of natural gas if only the price were right, were not only deemed heretical but were fought bitterly both by industry and Congress. By 1985 there had been a radical change in thinking brought about by the fall in the oil price. An IEA publication entitled "Natural Gas Prospects"gave an optimistic prognosis unthinkable ten years previously. Even at that time the authors, projecting the likely price of oil in the Year 2000 and thus the competing gas price, could not envisage the price of both being anywhere near as low as they actually became in that year.

But back in the heat of the crisis in the mid seventies, the prevailing mood in Congress was that if we can go to the Moon, we can certainly lick the energy problem. Money was thought to be the key to energy independence, and by the time I was Deputy Assistant Secretary for Energy Technologies in 1978 I myself had to defend a $3.8 Billion Energy research budget before the US Congress. That is not a mistake, it was billions. With a Congress pouring money into energy technologies without critical review, it is not surprising that some embarrassingly foolish initiatives were undertaken during that period. It was a great time for both "pork barrel" and perpetual motion machines! One by one, the large scale projects initiated in the late seventies succumbed to both large cost over-runs and non competitive products in the early eighties. Nevertheless, it is probably true that with alternative fuel supplies in the wings as an insurance policy, albeit with higher product prices, they did provide a threat of last resort to OPEC dominance. Not to have had such insurance would have been irresponsible.

There were, however, some notable successes which led to some major political and economic consequences. A major improvement in energy end use efficiency across the board was achieved through a combination of conservation practices, and improved technologies. The much maligned CAFÉ (Fleet average gas mileage targets) regulations forced manufacturers to rethink automobile designs with lighter weight materials and improved engine efficiency. Gas mileage in cars doubled, and this alone had a major effect on oil imports. The effects of energy conservation have been generally enduring because they were so widespread and pervasive, e.g. in gas heating furnaces and electric home appliances. Demand was thus being reduced at the same time that non-OPEC sources of oil were coming on line. The combination of the two meant that supply once again exceeded demand from OPEC sources. In 1985, the OPEC cohesion fractured, and it was forced to reduce its prices -- oil dropped from a peak of $40 per barrel of oil in 1980 towards $12 by the late nineties, each expressed in contemporary dollars. If one takes the high prevailing inflation rates into account, the feat of achieving this fall is even more impressive.

6. The Energy Technology Research Policy Dilemma.

I thus joined the IEA at a time in which energy matters generated political passions. There were two far reaching policy initiatives in place in 1980, which was my responsibility to bring to fruition. The first had been initiated by the Committee on Energy Research and Demonstration (CRD) in early 1976. It was an attempt to develop a "strategic view of new energy technologies from the standpoint of the overall energy needs and prospects for the IEA countries as a group". It was a wide ranging exercise, and was being brought to conclusion by my predecessor as I arrived on the scene briefly in February. It was left to me to provide the finishing touches, and these were approved by the Committee at its last meeting of the season in June of 1980. It was a stellar professional performance, but the strengths and weaknesses of any such study again rested largely upon the validity of out year oil price projections. This fact is driven home on the cover page of the Report designed by my colleague Niels de Terra. It was one of the first IEA reports to be published with a glossy graphic cover, and in this case it showed a graph with the worst and best scenarios for the years 2000 and 2020 in terms of IEA oil imports as a whole. Since both scenarios showed a reduction in future oil imports, and since neither has occurred in practice, one can safely say that both scenarios were optimistic. Scenarios for individual technologies were also predicated upon the future price of oil, and since this went down and not up in the out years it had a crucial effect upon the viability of most of the energy technologies. All the above eventualities were not obvious to the authors of the report at the time, excellent economists and scientists though they were, but the exercise illustrates once again the frailty of making projections in the out years based upon political imponderables. The effect is exacerbated when the bases for the predictions, such as the future price of oil, turn out later to be way outside the limits that any prudent person would have predicted at the time.

The second study was driven by another set of political considerations. The objectives were set at the highest levels of government, originating from the Tokyo (1979) and Venice (1980) Summit meetings. At the Venice meeting the Heads of State " reaffirmed their determination to maintain economic growth while reducing oil use. For the near and mid terms, emphasis was placed on conservation, and the expanded use of coal and nuclear power. For the longer term, substantial contributions from synthetic fuels and renewable resources of energy were also to be realized". Please note the reliance being placed on synthetic fuels being available in the future; in 1980, governments were prepared to place a high priority on achieving this goal.

As a result of this very direct expression of political will, a High Level Group was formed under auspices of the IEA which identified those individual commercial scale projects with a high probability of realization that were planned for completion by 1990. These projects were to include Tar Sands and Heavy Oils, Oils Shale, Coal Liquefaction and Gasification, New Coal Combustion Technologies, and fuels from Biomass and Liquid Fuels from Natural Gas. Such projects require resources in the range of billions of dollars each. A range of output levels was estimated for the year 2000 that were thought to be achievable if the technologies were be developed in the 1980s. Expectations were that fuels from these sources might reach between 5.0 million barrels of oil per day equivalent (mboe/d) and 11.6 mboe/d by the year 2000, or between 16% and 37% of estimated IEA oil imports in that year.

The study was certainly pushed vigorously by the Carter White House by high level emissaries, and sometimes their enthusiasm outstripped their diplomatic finesse. The tactics caused a certain amount of friction among the participants, of which I was reminded later by other governments. In 1980, the oil price seemed remorselessly headed higher and any thought to the contrary was unrealistic. The study was conducted, then, in good faith but based upon what turned out to be flawed premises. These remorselessly upward projections of the future oil price, which were used to justify the major investment in these alternative fossil fuel supplies, were to prove false. In 1985 when the oil price started to decline, it was obvious that synthetic fuels were not the same urgent necessity the Venice Summit considered them to be just five years previously. Furthermore, the incoming Administration of Ronald Reagan was philosophically opposed to what they considered industrial policy, and from being the subject of frenetic activity, the study was effectively put "on the shelf" early in 1981. A Report was finally considered by the Governing Board of the IEA on June 15 1981. It was perhaps significant that the cover of the Report is plain black as fits its unfortunate demise.

It proved to be a classic example of a major political dilemma -- in the face of a dire threat, as perceived by the Venice Summit, how much insurance do you take out in case that threat were to materialize? It seemed an imperative, at that time, to take out a level of insurance commensurate with the severity of the perceived threat to Western economies in case the oil price were, in fact, to move ever upwards--- what if it had?

Nevertheless, what happened to the few projects actually undertaken was unfortunate. The unilateral cancellation of some of projects envisaged in the Report, and which in fact were undertaken, such as Solvent Refined Coal Two, left some ruffled feathers on the part of several participating member governments, notably Germany and Japan. They were coping with already strained domestic budgets, and although in some sense they had "been let off the hook" budget wise by the cancellation, they felt they had embarked in good faith upon expensive international technology projects only to later to have those projects abruptly abandoned by the United States with little prior consultation. This unfortunate impression to some extent undermined the goodwill which had been essential in creating the IEA international energy projects, and I was reminded of those government's unhappiness frequently during the remainder of my tenure at the Agency. It affected the willingness of governments to enter fresh cooperative energy research agreements which were the mainstay of the IEA's Energy Research thrust.

7. Fables and Foibles.

The French are a richly blessed and talented people – the country seems to most visitors to function admirably. In short, France "works" -- but it is hard to see why since there are times when so few seem actually at work. French workers receive between five and six weeks paid holidays a year, and retire at age fifty-five on pensions equal to 97% of the pay of the working population. The Economist newspaper recently pointed out (Economist, 16th November 2002) that one result is that only thirty-seven per cent of the age bracket fifty-five to sixty-four remain in the labor market, compared with over two-thirds in Switzerland and Japan. These government provided pensions do not come out of some big fund: to the contrary the French have an almost religious belief in the principle of *"Répartition"*, which means that current pensions are entirely funded by current workers. It comes as no surprise that in France, government spending accounts for 53% of the Gross Domestic Product (GDP), as distinct from the OECD average of 38%. As if this were somehow deemed a hardship they also now have the benefit a thirty-five hour work week and ten public holidays associated with a variety of saints who they have much cause to bless.

We were to learn more about this public holiday largesse when we were planning to go to Switzerland on our first August vacation. We chose to leave on Friday, August 15[th,] which also happens to be a public holiday, Assumption Day. As a neophyte, I duly went to the bank just after noon on the 14th expecting to get both Swiss Francs and French

Francs. I had the somewhat naive notion that going to the bank the day <u>before</u> the Public Holiday would be a normal thing to do. But of course, my French friends told me, you should have known better; the bank was shut for good reason -- how else would they have time to prepare for going on holiday the next day, *C'est normal, n'est ce pas* ? I was left feeling the idiot I was intended to feel, but I was rescued on this occasion by my good friend Niels de Terra who magically produced quite enough Swiss Francs to do the trick.

France as an institution ceases to exist on the last weekend in July and resumes in the first week in September. Even the painter who was decorating our apartment had his own cottage in Normandy whence he retired for all August leaving our decorating project exactly as he left it, including the paint pots, until after the *rentreé*. The main roads in and out of Paris are predictably converted to large parking lots moving with glacial speed stretching to or from *la plage*. I remember with pain the scene in Lyon when I was foolish enough to attempt to cross it after eight o'clock in the morning during the *rentreé*. The entire city was carefully designed to close up like the bottom of a cardboard box; the result, instant paralysis. The archaic traffic layout of the City was compounded by the crafty french law of *priorité a drôite*. This law, invented by the devil himself, permits any traffic entering a roadway from the right to have priority over any vehicle on the principal road. This ensures that when one approaches a traffic circle it is perfectly easy to enter the circle but impossible to get out. The result is a state of gridlock that only the French could love; Lyon developed this traffic flow pattern to an art form.

One of the things the French are really very good at is advertising. The art work is superb, and the message is clear and to the point. One particularly sticks in my mind since it adorned nearly every bus stop shelter. It was for Boussin, the cream cheese. All you see is the two shapely legs of a young woman carrying a string shopping basket. In the basket are just three things; a *baguette*, a bottle of wine, and the distinctive square packet of "Boussin". All the caption says is " *Le Pain, le Vin, et le Boussin*". You assume, of course, that the young woman comes with it, and if she doesn't, with those legs she should. To be honest we felt that the advertisements on TV were often superior to the program content, and to our chagrin we learned much colloquial french from just watching the "ads" by themselves.

The French attitude towards the Law and its application was another instructive lesson. On the way to work up Boulevard Suchet, there were a number of "No left turn" signs. Those in the line of traffic flagrantly disregarded them, and as the offending motorist turned into the proscribed side road, he would merrily wave to the cop on the beat standing at the corner, who would salute back with equal cordiality. Very friendly to be sure, but something which would be unheard of in America where tickets would be issued like confetti. What was going on ? The answer lies in the attitude to the Law. In France, which follows the Napoleonic Code, the spirit of the Law is to be obeyed: in America the letter of the Law is what is important. If you are out late at night in America and come up to a Stop Sign, if your wheels do not actually stop you can be sure that a lurking police cruiser will nail you, even if there is nothing else on the road. In France, such a situation would be ignored, but woe betide you if you were to cause an accident in doing so – they would "throw the book at you". The law in France, then, is designed to resolve conflict: in America it is there to be obeyed---period!

The law is invoked in sometimes other curious ways. There was an unassuming blank brick wall near the apartment on a narrow back alley. The wall would not have been memorable but for one thing. Painted on the wall in a way which totally defiled it were the words " *Defense d'Afficher. Loi de Juilliet 26 1872*" or some such date. While making it illegal to paste an advertisement on a wall few people would normally pass, let alone see, it was not thought at all odd to paste an ugly notice forbidding such bill posting. Time and again we noticed such incongruous signs popping up to forbid you to do the unthinkable, each with the appropriate law generally stemming from the horse and cart era of the late 1800's. It reminds me of the alleged sign in the middle of a field which simply said :"It is illegal to throw stones at this Notice."

The French seem gluttons for punishment -- they appear enthralled with practical jokes even when they have to bear the brunt of them.

My favorite game is the national pastime called the gentle art of "*la petite grève*", or the little strike which is often no such thing.. The game is so much fun because it can be played with any number of players, at any time, at any place, and for any reason. A favorite time to play the game is when one is either leaving or arriving at an airport, and the immigration officers feel it's time to have some fun -- guess what ? Without warning they go on strike, leaving you in a line of people going nowhere. Isn't that neat? French passengers fume but understand even to the point of sympathizing with the plight of the poor officers; foreigners who seriously want to board planes , are bewildered and angry. All to no avail; some indeterminate time later the officials return, rested to be sure, and resume their mindless stamping of passports with renewed vigor. Everyone is relieved enough to go on his merry way rejoicing, and to allow his blood pressure to return to near normal.

Even more inconveniencing, is a *petite grève* on the Metro one line at a time and at rush hour. We experienced this on one occasion when, together with suitcases, we arrived at the *Gare de Lyon* by overnight train from Antibes. The seething mass of humanity invading the Metro would have dwarfed a football crowd, and the alternative way home was a circuitous route by bus. Naturally, the taxis were out in sympathy. Not surprisingly we were tired and irritable, which made us ripe for the belated discovery that Paris buses and suitcases don't mix too well. Although we ourselves were getting increasingly irritated, markedly absent from anyone else on the jammed packed bus was a remote sign of indignation; even touches of good humor emerged, usually absent from normal Parisian discourse. Our suitcases were tolerated with an air of good humored resignation, and were even carried down by some kind person to the curb for us. We concluded that it often takes a mini-crisis to bring the best out in Parisians.

To illustrate this last point of the French in a crisis mode, we were coming back to Paris on one occasion from *Fontainblau*, and were approaching a cross roads. To my consternation I suddenly saw a car coming towards me on my side of the road, but ten feet in the air over other cars in its path! It landed on its side with a horrendous noise, and the French really went to work. Everyone seemed to know exactly what to do, and oblivious to the fact that the thing might explode at any moment, they got all the occupants out fast and to safety. When all were seen to be safe, the crowd simply disappeared into thin air. It was a quite remarkable response.

Sometimes, however. this reputation is richly deserved. Truck drivers, for instance, have their own way of getting exactly what they want by using the finely honed technique of the *petit greve.* On some pretext, long forgotten by those who start the game, the truckers target the ring road around Paris, the *Péripherique.* It doesn't take very much normally to bring the *Peripherique* to a standstill, but these guys have got it to perfection. They get four mammoth *camions,* or trucks, and side by side they crawl at about ten kilometers an hour; there you have it, a moving *bouchon,* what fun! A bouchon is the cork in a bottle; it's also the name for a traffic jam. With four trucks driving abreast every few kilometers you have a pretty good idea of what the *Peripherique* looks like when this game is played. Although tempers tend to run high, the government gives in and the cracks in industrial peace are papered over.

Air France workers had a particular penchant for the strike weapon. Since the Government owned the airline at that time, compared to 54% today, the Government invariably capitulated rather than face the combined wrath of workers and traveling public, and even seemed to be apologetic to the workers for neglecting them so badly. It seems yet another case of where, because government spending touches the lives of so many people, the French public tends to sympathize more with public sector employees putting pressure on the government to "settle". The fact that Air France was hopelessly uneconomic with a mountain of debt was a matter of supreme indifference for, as usual, *"on s'arrange"* – the government conveniently pays off the debt, so everyone was happy. All, that is, except privately owned foreign airlines whose enlightened governments seemed quite willing to see them go bankrupt under identical circumstances.

As one noted earlier, France works very well indeed – when it is working.

8.   En Vacances.

New boys on the block have not normally accrued any serious vacation time, and I was no exception. Still, with the judicious use of those public holidays and weekends, I managed to have enough to have a memorable vacation with Helga. It was an opportunity for Helga to meet my Mother, Win, and my family. My Mother turned out to be an enthusiastic supporter of Helga from day one, and they maintained a wonderful relationship until Win died at the age of one hundred.

Helga duly took annual leave from the Government, and I met her at Gatwick Airport early on August 10th. With me to meet her was my brand new Peugeot of which I was very proud. It was my sister Doreen's Birthday, so we were able to have a good party. I think it was as good an introduction to an entirely strange family as one could get. After introducing Helga to a few country pubs, of which she approved mightily, Mother sported a dinner at a local hotel. Feeling well fed, and certainly well imbibed, we took our leave for France next day on the day ferry from Newhaven to Dieppe. It was a French tub of uncertain vintage, but today the Channel was calm and the crossing turned out to be a pleasant experience. Lest anyone think it is always like this, I have never been so sick in my life as on the English Channel. We had an excellent lunch on board, and four hours later we landed in Dieppe. Helga took over the new car on the two hour trip to Paris, and pronounced it to be to her satisfaction. What we would have done otherwise was anyone's guess, but I was so enamored with the car that it could have been the end of a beautiful friendship !

Helga also approved of the apartment, noting in her diary that it was "grand". In retrospect I think that was pushing it just a bit, but any complements were appreciated. I made one very major mistake – I had made everything too nice for her, and in my zeal to make it welcoming and attractive for her on her arrival, I had quite unconsciously appeared to have left her completely out of the loop and left no room for her to make a contribution to what, after all, was to be her home. Later, after some tears to be sure, we resolved that issue by throwing some things out, bringing some of Helga's very attractive furniture over in a second shipment of household goods in January, and of course embarking on some major joint purchases. Although the gaffe was totally unintentional it was non the less real and I took the lesson to heart. Strangely, it had a very positive outcome. We unwittingly established an important *modus vivendi* so that, to this day, everything in our home has been a sharing experience. We have had endless fun doing it that way.

August 14th was Helga's birthday, as it is most years. After we had had our little disappointment at the Bank, I phoned Niels to ask whether he had any ideas as to what to do. Nils had a stash of Swiss Francs, he said, and promised to come by later that afternoon. He and Bernd Kramer (from Bonn, who later became the German Science Counselor in Washington) duly arrived at the apartment for some dessert and a glass of champagne. The dessert proved a learning experience for Helga since she wanted to serve fresh cream with it. Accordingly she bought *crème fraiche* at the market and duly applied it liberally to the dessert. Her face put on a terrible grimace as she tasted it – it was as if it had turned sour. She made a major discovery, the first of many, that direct translations do not always work and that *crème fraiche* does not mean fresh cream

Helga had met Bernd previously in Washington, but it was the first time she had met Niels. Niels had spent a few weeks previously with the Deputy Executive Director of the IEA, Wally Hopkins. Wally sported a yacht in the Mediterranean which was his passion, and encouraged staff members with a yachting bent, like Niels, to come down for a week or two to help with crewing. Helga greeted Niels with her usual warm welcome, and with a classic malapropism we all shall never forget, said : "Hello Niels," she said, "how nice to meet you. I hear you have been screwing on a boat". A rather flustered Niels seemed to indicate that Helga's remark had rung a bell somewhere, but everyone had the good sense not to pursue this line of enquiry.

The next day we drove to Chambord, in the Loire Valley to take up the reservation I had made on the previous visit with Mother and Nigel in July. The Chateau dates from François Premier in the fifteen hundreds, and has to be one of the best story book chateaux in the world. It stands majestically in its moated meadows and standing beside it, as it were a little puppy, is the little Inn at which we were staying. It is a picture perfect setting. We had a room overlooking the Chateau, and the Dinner was true to form. There is no furniture at all in the Chateau, which is a great shame, but there is a remarkable central staircase wherein one spiral is wrapped around another. We were lucky enough to be there when there was a *Son et Lumiere* show. The spoken French was exceedingly dramatic, as was the illumination of this fine architectural masterpeice. We understood all too little of the presentation, but the final words were intoned in that deep french theatrical cadence which signifies high drama. "*Chambord. Reviens peut être. Oubliez jamais!*" It will be impressed on our memories forever; no Chambord, we will never forget you.

The next day we took slow secondary roads across France, over the Jura Mountains via Pontalier and into Switzerland. The weather deteriorated as be drove into Switzerland and up into the Lauterbrunen Valley. The village of Lauterbrunnen lies at the foot of an Alpine escarpment with the village of Mürren on its shelf, more than a thousand metres above the valley floor. Mürren was to be our home for the next week. No cars are allowed up in Mürren, so it has to be reached by a funicular mountain railway. It was now raining, and we had not eaten much during the day so we were famished and a little chagrined. A nearby hostelry offered a meal noteworthy not only because it was substantial, in typical Swiss fashion, but because it left the minimum impression on the taste buds. The car was duly parked safely near the entrance to the Bergbahn station, and we took the train to the top. It got foggier and foggier as we ascended, and you could not see your hand in front of your face when we finally got off. The other passengers scurried on their way and quickly disappeared as shadows into the fog, leaving us feeling suddenly very lost. John Evans had sent me some instructions on how to get to our vacation apartment, but with no light they were quite useless. I got the two suitcases, and followed the shadows into the fog thinking that they must at least be headed towards some form of habitation. In a short while we spotted the glimmer of a dim light doing its best to shine through the fog. Looking up at the building it was on, the lamp barely illuminated a sign which read "Sport Hotel". Whatever the term "sport" meant in this dismal context I was at a loss to know, but I did understand the word "hotel". That was quite enough for me. I dumped my increasingly heavy load smack in the middle of the road, and Helga remonstrated with me saying " Don't leave the bags there, some car will come and run over them". I grumbled something to the effect that "in the first place no cars are allowed in this village and, even if they were, no damn fool in his right mind would think of driving in this fog on a mountain like this" Helga seemed to accept this impeccable piece of logic, and the bags remained firmly in place in the middle of the road.

In what became a treasured, almost hallowed, family phrase ever since I invited Helga to "chat up the natives". This she did, to good effect. She disappeared into the hotel and soon reappeared beckoning me inside. I was only to happy to pick up the deserted bags and follow her in. I was relieved to discover that the hotel staff not only understood Helga's German but that they chatted back with considerable animation. Whereas a few minutes before we seemed hopelessly lost in the fog, now we had a room for the night. This was a development with great implications – it meant that this nincompoop with no language ability now had a first rate linguistic ally. I had always thought of Helga in a strictly English speaking American context, and to hear her speak fluent German was a pleasant revelation. But when we visited England, who was it who was going to "chat up the natives"? That, as Hamlet would have said, is the rub

It turned out to be an excellent hotel with a charming room, so we counted our blessings. The next morning it was still foggy, but at least one could see something of the road ahead. We could now read the instructions as to where to find our vacation apartment, and we showed these to the concierge. He knew where it was, and arranged for a porter to accompany us to our destination with a mechanized cart. With memories of the weight of the bags still fresh in my mind from the night before, the cart was a godsend. We trudged through the village for about ten minutes or more until we duly arrived at the place where the key was to be retrieved. Grateful for the help, we at last found our little nesting box for the week. It was still foggy, so the surroundings remained a mystery. All things considered, there are worse things in life than to be holed up, alone together and in love, in the fog in a Swiss Chalet. We would just have to get used to it !

The apartment proved to be in a three storied condo chalet. It was furnished pleasantly but not lavishly, as is true of many mountain homes including our own in the Blue Ridge Mountains of Virginia. The chalet had a series of picture windows in the living room overlooking a balcony, but since the fog still annoyingly hung around, there was still no view. We had seen a small grocery store as we had approached the chalet, and so we stocked up with food for lunch and dinner. We also made another discovery – we had come up to M_rren at the wrong end of the village, and by the wrong means. Right next to the grocery was a fine modern cable car station. It was, apparently a half way station to the Schilthorn, which features in one of the James Bond movies with memorable snow scenes.. Thus we had to retrace our steps once more through M_rren, and go down on the funicular to retrieve our parked car in Lauterbrunnen. Then we then drove along the valley to the little village of Steckelberg where the cable car station below our chalet was located. We parked the car once more and, feeling somewhat foolish, ascended the stark three thousand foot face of the cliff in the gondola to reach the spot where we should have been the night before!

Towards late afternoon, the fog had lifted sufficiently to see that we were perched almost perilously close to the edge of the escarpment, and could make out the dark walls of the other side of the Lauterbrunnen

Valley. Interesting though this sight was, it merited not much more than a contented yawn. Then, towards evening, it happened – something quite magic. As if we were sitting in the orchestra stalls of a theater, the curtain of fog slowly lifted before our eyes, and there before us stood the magnificent sight of one of the most majestic ranges of mountains in the world, the Alpine chain of the Jungfrau, the M_nch, and the Eiger. The picture windows in the Chalet were there for a purpose after all ! As the fog drew away, it revealed the snow capped peaks against a cloudless blue sky, and as the sun went down the pink rays painted the mountains with *"Abend rot"*. The Swiss Railways had published a picture of this wonderful sight, and we have it framed to this very day in our home, a constant reminder of that perfect first vacation

It occurred to me during this scenic reverie, that my daughter-in-law Debbie was expecting her child right about that time, and there should be some way we could find out about it. International phone calls were still a mystery to most Swiss at that time, and the only way seemed to be to go into Interlaken to the post office. PTT, was the umbrella organization run by the most European governments in Europe to combine the functions of postal services, telegraphs and telephones. They would have a stranglehold on progress for years to come, and the thought of privatization was yet a radical idea in the devious mind of some revolutionary somewhere. The post office was an imposing building close to the *bahnhof*, since the Swiss PTT had an incestuous relationship with the railroads in Switzerland as they also had with the busses. In fact busses used to have little boxes on their sides where one could actually mail letters, as well as racks on the back of them to which you can attach your bicycle! We managed to find a most helpful attendant, and booked a call to my Mother. She was overjoyed to hear us, and told us that I had a little grandson. Figuring out the time difference, we decided to be really extravagant and place a call to Martin in America to congratulate him. "You can dial yourself", said the attendant. "*Null, null, eins ,eins*" she intoned. We were deeply impressed with the modern technology which even the Swiss now appeared to have, and duly entered the cabin to place the call. What was it "null, null something........" A sleepy Martin answered the phone, and we heard that everything had gone very well and that

Debbie and the baby were doing fine. He also informed us that the baby was to be named "Eric" – not too bad an idea when you think about it ! We walked lightheartedly back to our car, and I reminded Helga that this meant that she was getting involved with a grandfather, which would make her an instant grandmother! As I recall, she took the news without noticeably flinching---a great effort at self control.

Grindelwald has to be one of the most idyllic of Alpine villages, and the place is smothered in color from the prolific display of flowers: even the buffers at the bahnhof have boxes of geraniums in them. Although picturesque in Summer, it is a naturally a very popular center for skiing in Winter. The *First Bahn* is a chair lift that takes you up in four stages to the high plateau at seven and a half thousand feet where the skiing must be magnificent. There is the inevitable restaurant at the top which serves hot snacks and one can swill one's beer while admiring the stunning view of the *Ober Grindelwald Gletcher* on the far side of the Grindelwald Valley. Have you ever been on vacation to a remote idyllic spot, such as this one was, and bumped into stereotypes who you thought, and wished, that you had left behind at home ? For instance, a "yobo" from Liverpool spewing forth invective in some form of the English vernacular that would make the Beetles blush ? – or the corpulent and highly vocal German who would be more at home in a life-long Oktoberfest complete with "oompapas"? In this case, the two we met happened to be Americans of uncertain provenance who came straight out of central casting for Archie Bunker. Their voices were as loud and shrill as the their utterances were vacuous – Helga and I immediately gave them the names of "Flo" and "Harry", and this couple have come to represent two mythical characters which we invoke to describe persons who we meet from time to time – but would rather not. We met one such person on a ship recently who ranted and raved in a voice which reverberated around the Dining Room about some taxi driver in France who had the effrontery of declining his dollar bill---he was a "Harry", but mercifully without a "Flo"!

It turned out that my old friend from Radiocarbon days, Hans Oeschger had an apartment in a chalet in *Grindelwald*. It was on a small road leading up into the alpine meadows, with magnificent scenery. We hiked up to the *Ober Grindelwald Gletscher* with its pale saphire blue ice. Helga, always direct, asked about the nature of the geology of the rocks at that point. Hans and I were in some doubt, and fluffed the issue. Hans later did some research on it when he got back to Bern, and it turned out to be a limestone which was hard up against the granite of the massif, so there was some complexity to it after all. Helga was allowed her chuckle over the fact that two geophysicists didn't know the difference between the two rocks, but then we argued that she didn't either so we didn't feel too bad about it!

Hans, who was a Professor at the University of Bern, was by this time a noted Swiss scientist, and he kindly arranged for us to obtain *"Specialbillet für Forscher"*. (Special free ticket for Scientists) on the Jungfrau Railway which takes one to the *"Jungfraujoch"*, which is nearly at the top, at twelve thousand feet. The journey is in two stages and takes a whole day. The first stage is as far as *"Kleine Scheidegg"* where you change trains before embarking on the really serious climb to the summit. The sweeping expanse of the *Aletsch Gletscher*, as it curves its way down the valley like a giant highway, is a great reward as you leave the train. It is breathtaking sight, literally, since the altitude got to you in short order. The train wends its way downward again across the lush green pastures of the *"Wengen Alp"*. The train schedule allows you to stop off at *Wengen* for coffee and cream cake before finally descending into the *Luatenbrunnen* Valley. It was the terrain we could see from our chalet on the other side of the Valley, and it all seemed to come straight out of a travel brochure. This panorama adorns the bathroom at our small farm in Virginia

We had many more enjoyable moments in the Bernese Oberland, but all good things must come to an end and we had to return home to Paris. What a wonderful image "home to Paris" conjures up, and for the next five years we were to cherish that image. We drove by a more direct Autoroute to Paris, stopping on the way for a picnic beside the highway. Helga had bought some supplies the night before, and set about preparing the lunch using the hood of the Peugeot as a convenient table. I stared in wide eyed amazement as Helga absentmindedly cut the sandwiches with an audible scratching, grinding, noise using a serrated bread-knife directly on the metal of the hood. She shamefacedly realized what she was doing – and on my new car too ! Oh dear! This scar, fortunately small, was still there as a reminder of that wonderful vacation, and the picnic on the Autoroute, until we left France in 1985.

There was some unfinished energy related business in Washington associated with the High Level Review about which I have commented earlier, so by good fortune I was able to accompany Helga back to the States. This gave us the chance to get some domestic things in order and, more importantly perhaps, lay plans for our immediate and longer term future. There were so many practical steps to take, and so many momentous decisions to make. We were in for a very busy time. I was due to go on what turned out to be a round-the world trip in late September via Tokyo, Helga would come over for a week in October to get the lay of the land, I would come over for Christmas with my Mother, Helga would resign from the Civil Service, and she would then join me in Paris permanently in mid-January. Close friends were by now coming to know what was happening, and that we were now *á deux*. The cheerful acceptance of that fact was encouraging beyond measure---the "what took you so long" question was hard to answer, for there wasn't one. The few days also gave us the opportunity to make a quick trip to Ohio to see the newborn, Eric Jr. It was a happy event, as indeed it should have been. We went out again to Ohio in June of 2002, this time to see him graduate from Ohio University. Another Ohio trip saw him married to Meghan, and yet another to introduce us to our new and first grandson! We were immensely proud on each occasion, and thought back fondly to those very early days. How time flies !

I eventually left to go back to Paris on Labor Day. It was baking hot at Dulles, and we were flying on a TWA L1011. It was so hot in fact that the pilot announced that there was not enough weight of fuel on board to make the crossing. Faced with falling either into the Atlantic or waiting till the plane cooled off, we opted for the delay with reasonable grace as the bar was opened. Nevertheless, I was disturbed by the narrowness of the margin when it came to fuel!

9.   Tokyo...............and beyond

At its last meeting of the Committee for Research and Development before the summer recess, the Japanese Government had presented a formal invitation to hold the next meeting in Tokyo. There was some grumbling from some of the European delegates, principally because they were worried that they may not get travel funds, but the Japanese countered by saying that they were the ones who always had to find the travel funds and who always had to come that long distance from Japan to Paris. Their rationale prevailed, and the date was set for late September. This was certainly an opportunity both to see something of Japan, and to visit other parts of the Orient. The prevailing mood was one of intense anticipation.

Niels de Terra, Peter Dyne from Canada and I agreed to meet up in Hong Kong a few days in advance. I was booked First Class on a Cathay Pacific flight out of London, Gatwick. Up in the quiet nose of a 747, the world looked pretty good. The day was fine, and I recognized the terrain all the way to Frankfurt. After Frankfurt, lunch was served complete with a rose in a specimen glass on the well manicured tablecloth. Cathay Pacific knows how to treat one well, at least in First Class, served graciously by the Chinese stewardesses whose pulchritude is legendary The next stop was Istanbul, where we picked up more passengers for Bahrein. On the way, we passed over Iraq, and it turned out that we were the last plane to pass over Basra before hostilities between Iraq and Iran broke out with a vengeance. Better than being the first plane _after_ hostilities broke out!

The section out of Bahrein was the night flight over India: it is a matter of regret that although I have flown over the sub-continent many times, I have never set foot on it. The plane circled over Canton before descending into the old Hong Kong Airport of Kai Tak, and one could see the rice paddy fields along the flood plain. From the air, one is quite detached from the culture and people on the earth below. Who were they, and what were they doing this minute, these people whose country, in 1980, I could not visit nor could they come to mine. And yet we were so close, two miles apart spatially but a million miles in reality. I was a mere space ship visiting this planet of theirs on a fly by mission.

This philosophical speculation was cut short by the quick descent into Kai Tak, which had a very sporty approach whose thrills many veteran fliers will miss − it passed between two mountain peaks, with people in high rise apartments staring out of their windows at you as you fly by. After resting up at the hotel in Kowloon I met up with the other two to find an authentic Chinese restaurant, not the chow-mein version which appears in every town in America. Niels had one such in mind, and assured us that this would be just fine Peter and I had a few misgivings as we spied buckets with just barely live fish of dubious age near the entrance. Sure enough, after ordering a fish dish, a non too hygienic looking cook made his way to the entrance, and came back with fish of uncertain ancestry flapping about in his hand. There were some apprehensive looks around the table, but when they arrived cooked, we had to admit that they tasted pretty delicious. We had a further day in the City, which has to be one of the most vibrant in the world. Taking the ferry from Kowloon to Victoria Island is a real thrill because the Harbor is always full of a mixture of small junks and tall ships through which the ferry manages to weave its way. I had been there once some six years previously, and could hardly recognize the profile of the City, since huge sky scrapers now stood in place of very modest buildings earlier. Four years later, the skyline had leaped ahead yet again and who knows what it must be like today.

In the morning I was to catch the JAL flight to Tokyo, and I became quite intrigued by the Kowloon hotel check out procedure. Bags were stacked in one corner of the foyer guarded by a bell hop, and nobody was not allowed to depart with one's bag before one had shown proof of having paid the bill. There were several highly vocal arguments held out in the open foyer, and the charade was obviously designed to embarrass the hell out of some characters who sheepishly retraced their steps to the Cashier's desk. It must have said something about the clientele, and I thought it was an upscale hotel !

The Tokyo flight was about three and a half hours, and one forgets just how long distances are in that part of the world. We landed in what was then the new Tokyo Airport of Narrita, which proved to be away out in the sticks and the ride into the City air terminal on the bus took for ever. The old one, Haneda, was situated on Tokyo Bay just south of Yokohama, and was much more convenient. This was now closed to international traffic to cope with the burgeoning domestic trade. Reservations had been made for us in customary efficient Japanese style at the Grand Palace Hotel, at the edge of the Imperial Palace grounds. I had a room on the 19th floor, with a magnificent view. All our documentation awaited us, and no detail was left undone. There was a cordial welcome reception with dinner at the hotel in the evening, and we retired early feeling that although we had had a good but exhausting day, tomorrow was one full of promise.

It was at four o'clock in the morning when I had the awful feeling of someone walking over my bed with boots on. No one should have the bad manners to be walking over anyone's bed, I sleepily reasoned, let alone with his boots on. It took a few moments to regain consciousness and get my senses together. I then realized that this must be an earthquake, my first of any note. It was indeed. The furniture seemed to want to move around the room in random fashion, the bathroom fittings rattled like castanets, and when I got out of bed the floor wanted to dance with me. Japanese hotels are built to withstand these things, I reassured myself hopefully, but at four in the morning I found that great insight to be of little comfort. I was on the 19th floor, after all, and the building was waving about like an upside down pendulum, creaking and groaning in an arthritic rhythm. The earthquake passed, but a waving building which is designed to wave does not have its oscillations damped that quickly. I have no idea of the actual duration, but the creaking and groaning seemed to go on forever. I eventually went to the window to look out onto a Tokyo which I expected to see in total ruins, but all was quiet in the streets below, although they looked a disconcertingly long way down from the 19th floor. I eventually feel asleep again, and woke up remembering my awful dream. When the others in the morning recounted the same awful dream, I began to take this matter more seriously. It was reported in the paper next day as being about magnitude 5.2, *pas grand chose* as the French would say, but there had been fatalities in a village way outside Tokyo. It was even more of a surprise, though, to have exactly the same thing happen the next night, at exactly the same time, as if it had been computer programmed. We now had a valid statistical observation based on two nights stay: earthquakes occur in Tokyo every night at four in the morning! Luckily, the third night was without incident, and our theory was mercifully discredited. I put through a call to Helga in Washington to tell her of my heroic experiences and miraculous escape, but the only earthquakes she was concerned about were at work at the FCC, which happen there regularly on a daily basis!

The next day was free before the meetings began, and an intrepid few of us took the opportunity to explore the Tokyo Metro system. All the Metro maps were of course in Japanese, but there is a strange thing about Metro maps the world over. With the constant exposure to the pressure from the fingers of curious travelers, the station of origin has nearly always been obliterated, leaving a rather grubby blob on the map. This is Home Base ! This is true whether the Metro is in Washington, Tokyo, London, Paris, Montreal, Rome or Moscow. Even if you cannot read it, you can make out where you are. In Tokyo, all one had to do was to memorize the Japanese station names by pattern recognition, and you were in business. So far so good, but it turned out that the Metro system is cut up into, and run by, separate independent companies. It was not possible to get a ticket from one destination to another with an interchange involving lines owned by different companies. You have to buy a separate ticket along the way. Successive refusals at ticket barriers with gesticulations punctuated by staccato grunts in Japanese finally got this idea across to us, and I must say we were helped on our way by some helpful Japanese who spoke English.

Tokyo is one of the worlds great cities: it is exciting and vibrant and compelling to visit -- yet at that time it would have been hard to call it appealing. It was big, busy, noisy, full of undistinguished buildings and choked with people and traffic. Utility came before aesthetics. Pollution to be sure was getting under control, and the people in the streets had shed their protective masks. When I returned five years later one could even see across Tokyo Bay. Nevertheless, one saw little beauty in the same way one sees it in a Buenos Aires, for instance. There are no wide boulevards and no memorable vistas, with the exception of the area around the Imperial Palace which is immaculately kept. Its suburbs were drab and nondescript, and ran into each other interminably. From reports in the newspaper today, many old buildings have been torn down and gleaming new architectural wonders have replaced them. I would certainly like to see the revitalized city.

The commuter railroads are a nightmare and perpetually jammed packed. At the Tokyo rail terminals men with conspicuously hygienic white gloves push people in to get one more soul aboard. We came to the conclusion after several visits over the next five years that it must be quite difficult being a Japanese government official. Every office in the Ministry of International Trade and Industry, MITI, appeared to have a similar layout. The Director, his Deputy, and their assistants worked in a line of desks with their backs to the window. The "worker bees" work at three or four rows of back to back desks at right angles to the windows. Our government official, a well educated and experienced professional, usually lives in the outer suburbs with an hour and a half commute. When he does get home it is usually late at night because conscientiousness is valued very highly for promotions -- we saw cots placed in offices for all night stays. If he were to go home it would be to a pricey apartment with minimum floor space. I have only once been invited to a Japanese home, and that was more or less by accident. The wife was from the well to do family of Mikimoto pearls, and they were able to afford an attractive but modest sized apartment in Akasaka, a relatively high rent district. Japanese make up for the lack of home entertaining by being extremely hospitable in dining out. Here you can be treated lavishly, almost embarrassingly so, because you know how much all this is costing. Restaurants were so dreadfully expensive that one ate in places like tempura bars . This was by no means a hardship, for tempura served by the cook over the counter straight from the boiling pot of oil is one of my delights. As hosts, the Japanese are careful to study your likes and dislikes, and report back. On one later visit to Tokyo, Helga and I were met in the hotel lobby by a senior Japanese official, Ambassador Kazuhiko Togo, the grandson of the famous Admiral of that name. He greeted us with "Eric, I hear you like tempura, there's a splendid place just here". How did he know !?

The Japanese were impeccable hosts and we were treated, if that be the word, to a special Japanese tea party ceremony not accorded to many foreigners. Ceremony is the correct word, for a party it was not. It is difficult to be charitable in describing this ordeal. One has to sit very patiently cross legged on the floor while the noxious mixture is brewed. Americans and Europeans do not seem anatomically suited to this posture, and for them the position is excruciatingly uncomfortable. After interminable steps, each with its ritual of incantations, the frothy green tea is then proffered around, one person at a time so there can be no hiding one's reaction. It tasted far worse than it even smelled – it was astringent and quite awful The temptation to spit it out before God and everybody was almost overwhelming, but protocol dictated otherwise. We have one such polished tea making chest from Japan in our home to this day, which is a treasured possession of ours. It has a lined box-like cavity for the coals which heat the utensils, and little drawers for the implements and tea caddies, but while lovely to look at it will never be used !

Tsukuba is a new science city built about fifty miles out of Tokyo. On this my first visit it was largely incomplete, but a mere five years later all the vacant tracts of land we saw on this occasion were occupied by large buildings. The city was mature enough to host an immense Worlds Fair and plenty of modern scientific institutes. The investment had been huge---there was a high energy physics laboratory rivaling anything in the other IEA countries. On the social side, we were greatly perplexed when we visited a fish restaurant in Tokai Mura because we were offered large fried fish which we were supposed to eat with chop sticks. There were a lot of furtive glances around the room to see how best to accomplish this feat, and fingers were called into play as a last resort. I am still not sure how to do it decorously to this day.

The CRD meetings were held at the Ministry of International Trade and Industry. They were well organized, and our hosts were impeccable with their arrangements. One of our principal hosts was Madame Kauwaguchi from the Foreign Ministry who was later to become Japan's Foreign Minister. Gracious as she is competent, she was one of many colleagues we were to come to hold in the highest regard. The Japanese system of screening and training provides a cadre of professionals who are first class. While we were in Tokyo, Leslie Boxer and I were invited to interview a man designated to be the new Japanese member of our staff in Paris. It turns out that "interview" is a curious word for the process. By Western standards it was a non-interview because the decision had already been made in Tokyo, and we were there to get to know him, not to approve of him. Frankly, I had been dissatisfied with the performance of his predecessor who had regarded Paris as a playground, and I had made this evaluation known when asked directly by the a member of the Japanese Embassy in Pari – they pulled him at once, and this young man we were 9nterviwing was his replacement. We should have had no concerns about this man's qualifications for he turned out to be an excellent addition to our staff. His name was Mishiro and he was a PhD Physicist of no mean achievement who later rose to high rank in MITI. I was later to be very glad both for his scientific acumen and his wise counsel, and also for his ability to maintain the vital smooth relations with the Japanese delegation to the IEA and our office. But at this moment he was at a blackboard polishing up his French, which was a nice gesture but Leslie and I were looking for more technical qualifications. The incident highlighted the cultural differences in the recruitment process between those practiced in the West and those peculiar to the Orient, and I was to learn that both had to be respected if one is to succeed in international organizations.

Eric H. Willis

From being Fall in Tokyo it was Springtime when I arrived in Sydney on the ten and a half hour overnight Qantas flight. I grabbed a taxi to the Hyatt Kingsgate Hotel where I had stayed before. This hotel has about the finest view of downtown Sydney, the Harbor and the Opera House that you could wish for. I checked in, and the receptionist asked me for my address. I said "Arlington, Virginia, USA", and this evoked some self conscious chuckles and a faint blush from the young lady. I could not imagine anything at all funny about this prosaic statement, for most foreigners have heard of Arlington and its famed Cemetery. When I came to check out the next day, however, my address on the bill stared me in the face; it read " Arlington, Vagina, USA". I really ought to learn to speak Australian and avoid those pitfalls.

I walked down to the Harbor area via the very attractive Botanic Garden and reached the point where the ferry boats depart. At that time it was still a bit grotty and rundown, with the old immigrant boarding houses still in place. A few years later this was transformed into a gleaming upscale waterfront. The boats depart from the inner harbor which lies wedged between the famous Harbor Bridge and the now even more famous Opera House. Leaving the inner harbor area on the hydrofoil to Manley, the view of the Opera House with the Harbor Bridge as a backdrop remains a vivid memory, and exhilarating would not be too strong a word. I was able to take a series of telephoto shots from the boat as we passed the Opera House, and I have them framed on the wall in my study right now as a constant reminder of that Spring day.

From being a white elephant, the Opera House is now the crown jewel of Sydney. The architect was much maligned because no one could figure out how to get the roof on, and the City Fathers nearly gave up on it when they faced a huge prospective financial loss – in an act of faith they kept going, and they were richly vindicated. There was not a scheduled performance on that evening, but there was instead a charity fund raiser for young up and coming Australian and New Zealand artists. The lead singer, as a drawing card, was a young woman called Kiri te Kanawa. Since that evening her fame as an opera star has spread far and wide, but then she was relatively unknown. The evening gave me a more protracted opportunity to look around this architectural wonder, with its sail like roof and sweeping lines which have become the icon of a great city.

Canberra, Australia's capital, is a city built by and for government. One could say that it has been largely successful, although it is hard to get away from the company town syndrome entirely. While many mistakes were made, its decentralized plan involving discrete communities really seems to work. I was there at the invitation of the Australian representative to the CRD, Tom McMahon to meet with the Energy Ministry staff. The meetings were held, in part, at the Australian National University, ANU, where coincidently my old Cambridge friend Donald Walker headed a Pacific Studies Center in the Geography Department. I stayed with Donald and his family in their home. He arranged for a most jovial party, and invited some old friends from Cambridge days who I had never expected to see again in my life.

No visit to Canberra would be complete without a visit to the nature reserve at Tidbinbilla. There the kangaroos are free to roam around, and Koala Bears sleep high in the eucalyptus trees. The "pub" at Gundaroo is another but different bone fide Canberra attraction which only the hardy would appreciate. A bus load of people sets off in the evening around seven, and heads out into the outback seemingly forever. Eventually, in the middle of nowhere, one arrives at a tumble down wooden structure where the fire was going and the barbecues were ready for their burnt offerings. The menu was simple, just three items; enormous steaks, baked potatoes and lots, and lots, and lots of beer. The eating and drinking lasted until midnight, when a fairly inebriated bunch boarded the bus for home, singing their heads off until slumber took over. What an evening !

One thinks of New Zealand as being on Australia's doorstep, but Sydney is as far from Auckland as Washington is from Denver. New Zealand has a special magic about it. Whereas Australians often come across as being a bit up tight, New Zealanders seem the epitome of relaxation. I feel instinctively at home there and, as luck would have it

, I have managed four visits there in various incarnations. My first stop was to Wellington, New Zealand's Capital. I wanted very much to see my old Cambridge friends Pat Suggate, then Director of the Geological Survey, and Athol Rafter, Director of the Institute for Nuclear Studies at Lower Hutt. Nevertheless, my prime objective was to meet with the Heads of New Zealand Electricity and Shell Exploration who had their headquarters in Wellington. The Maui gas field, one of the largest in the world, was just being developed and there were various proposals for its use, some highly controversial. I had been more than flattered when the New Zealand Energy Department had solicited my thoughts on the subject. Although I thought I had firm appointments, both men were said to be "out of town" when I arrived at their offices. Somehow communications in the Government's liaison process had broken down, and I had to be content talking to some pleasant people below the policy level: despite their kindness in receiving me the discussions tended to be somewhat vacuous. I was greatly disappointed because it meant that that part of my mission would be a failure – in short, it was a "bummer". The next day was a Saturday, and Athol asked me what I would like to do most . I said I would like to watch a cricket match at the famous Wellington Cricket Ground, from which I remember hearing crackling radio commentaries way back in my boyhood. He said he too would very much like to do that, and it would have been his first choice for he was a member. It was such a picturesque setting, the game was good, and I settled down for a pleasant afternoon with "no worries". At the tea interval Athol and I went into the pavilion to have a welcome "cuppa". You can imagine my astonishment when I was introduced to the two men I had come all this way to meet! They too were members of the Wellington Cricket Club! They were most apologetic about what had happened, and were quite willing to give me their views on the subject of the Maui Gas Field, which was heavy on the minds of both. So I managed, after all, to talk with precisely the right people, all seated together at one time, and in the most convivial of settings!

My next stop was Auckland, which I had visited once before. I had met Garth Harris and his wife Margaret on that trip, and formed a lasting friendship. Garth now had an energy group associated with the university concentrating on alternative energy sources and their utilization, and took a prominent role in trying to get natural gas from the Maui field used in automobiles. This would not only be clean fuel, but would save New Zealand a lot of hard currency. New Zealanders seem to enjoy life, and the Harris' have a second home on an island in the bay and naturally a yacht to go with it. Pleasant though this visit was, I was soon preoccupied by the logistics of getting home ! Air New Zealand was threatening to go on strike that evening, and I was glued to the TV in the hotel room for the latest news. They actually did strike an hour or so later, and there were apparently no planes out. Pan Am had no space either, and I left the hotel phone number as a long shot. I then booked, and paid for, a further night's stay and offered the Harris's, who had come to the hotel to fetch me, a kind of consolation dinner. Somehow Pan Am phoned the hotel and got in touch with me about 9.30pm to say that they had a seat on their flight leaving at 11pm. We promptly gathered all my belongings from the room and made a somewhat undignified exit. The Harris's made a mad dash to the airport with me, leaving a good meal and an empty paid for bed behind.

It was a straight shot to Los Angeles with a refueling stop in Hawaii. Since there was a strike on, the food suppliers had honored the picket lines, so there was neither food nor booze on board. No worries, as they say "down under". I had planned through the airline to stay the night in Los Angeles overnight, have a good night's sleep, and take the day plane to Washington. I would call this the sane scenario. Driven by the imponderable forces associated with the word "Love", I chose the insane scenario which involved flying on the "red eye" for the second consecutive night. Helga picked up this absolute wreck at 6am at Dulles Airport, and I seemed quite *non compus mentis* -- some lover boy! Of course, I had gained very little in actual fact because I slept solidly all day while Helga worked all day, so it was a zero sum game. But recovery with Helga did not take all that long, and it was a great couple of days.

A rare thrill was in store for me on the last leg back to Paris. For a few hundred dollars, at that time, you could upgrade from First Class on Air France to the Concorde, and this I had done. The plane left at 2.00pm Washington time, and by a time change quirk we arrived three and a half hours later in Paris Charles de Gaulle at 10pm Paris time – time enough to sleep in one's own bed instead of the "red eye". The plane is well appointed but long and narrow, with two seats either side of the aisle and tiny, tiny windows. The service was as good as it is cracked up to be, with a succession of exotic courses. Flying at sixty thousand feet, the sky is quite black when you look upward. The take-off roar is powerful, and there is another slight rumble when it goes through the sound barrier. I thought it all quite marvelous, and a beautiful end to a fascinating round the world trip.

Well, not quite – the fun hadn't finished yet. After taking a sleeping pill because of the time change and the whirlwind rate of travel, not to mention work in the morning, I blissfully dozed off. I do have some recollection in the recesses of my mind that while in a semi-conscious daze I received a phone call from the United States. I have no recollection of what was said or who said it, but I do know that the next month's France telecom bill faithfully recorded both the fact and the time, 3 am, together with a "call collect" charge of one hundred dollars. So much for taking the Concorde in the hope of dodging the overnight "red - eye", and getting a good night's sleep.

10. Helga's Reconnoitering Foray.

At home here in Arlington, Virginia, October can be a most pleasant month with sunshine and blue skies. Columbus Day on October 12th is the highpoint of the foliage in the Blue Ridge. By contrast, October in Paris can be quite miserable, and this one was no exception. If Helga had been coming on a week's sight seeing purely for pleasure, she would have been sadly disappointed. It was cold, wet, and generally inhospitable. The owners of the apartments in our building vote each year to turn on the central heating on October 15th, and not a day before. What do you do if it is cold before that time? The answer is simple— you freeze. Added to which, when the heat does come on, air rises upward through the system to the top floors. Since you could not go any higher than our apartment, we got the air in our radiators instead of hot water. Nobody bothered to tell us this, so we went on freezing until Helga, coming to grips with the reality of Paris living rather than the romantic version, complained bitterly to the Concierge who arranged for the radiators to be bled. Once heat was restored, the reverse situation prevailed, and you could fry an egg on the radiators

The Concierge, Madame Sanier, became Helga's firm friend. She was born in Calais, and was also born street wise. She had a keen eye for human nature, and was nobody's fool. When she knew something on someone, she would put her finger under her eye, and pull down the eyelid a fraction as if to say " I'm not telling, but………". Then she told you ! We came to have a great affection her, for she was the genuine article and the number of favors she would do for you were endless. She lived in a small efficiency apartment at the entrance to the building, and monitored closely the passers by from her window. After we were back in America for about five years, we heard that she had had heart bypass surgery and was in hospital near the *Porte d'Orleans*. By chance we were visiting Paris during her recovery, and I will never forget the look on her face as we entered her room, "*Mon Dieu, c'est n'est pas vrai ....*" she cried, and the three of us burst into tears of joy. That was friendship: she was one of those fine people one meets throughout life one is glad to have known !

Getting to know how to shop was a key objective. Helga explored the supermarket which wa s close to the apartment, but mercifully half hidden underground. It modestly called itself the Euromarché, and it was always crowded. Unlike its American equivalents, its presentation was more utilitarian than attractive. The floors were worn, often littered with bits of paper; it offered more of a convenient resource than a pleasurable experience. The cosmopolitan clientele was perfectly in keeping with the ambiance, and the air quality inside consistent with both. Helga soon found that the check out lines posed a real challenge, with people jumping the line as if it were a sport. The French will grumble about these things, but never seem to take the initiative and do anything about it. Helga thought differently, and prodded one aging miscreant to get his surprised attention and said loudly, "*Aprés moi, monsieur!*". Not only did the wretch retreat to the back of the line, but the rest of the line applauded! I could see that Paris shopping and Helga were made for each other, and that she might even have a beneficial effect on the Quartier.

No, the pleasures of food shopping in Paris, and there are many, lie in the markets and the small shops of the *Quartier*. The open markets are a special feature: they have all the fresh produce one could wish for and the fish, some with their gills still moving, come straight in from the ports every day. The variety of species, from both the Atlantic and the Mediterranean, is overwhelming, and the prices are relatively reasonable. When it came to fruit and vegetables, however, Helga found them somewhat expensive—welcome to the European

Common Agricultural Policy !. She reported that she did not consider
the stall holders unfriendly, nor were they particularly friendly either;
they tended to conduct their business with an air of armed neutrality.
Later, when her French had improved to the point of swearing both
volubly and fluently, she was able to go toe to toe with the stall holders,
and this improved the pleasure of shopping immeasurably – she got
used to the "*non, Madame, on ne touche pas*" and went on doing so
anyway. The market opened twice a week come rain or shine about a
hundred yards from the apartment, and in winter oil lamps would offer
a cheerful glimmer of light to the scene. After the hustle and bustle of
the morning, the sidewalk was cleared away and hosed down by two
o'clock as if nothing had ever happened.

The shops in the immediate *quartier* provided the basics, and
contrary to expectations they embraced us as part of their family after
a while. The *boulangérie* was run by two delightful ladies, always neatly
dressed in trim pink frocks. At seven in the morning that luscious of
all aromas, freshly baked french bread, would waft down the boulevard
towards you, and your gastric juices would work overtime. The ladies'
way of doing business was a little old fashioned in some ways. For
instance, if you wanted your loaf of bread sliced, you would be charged
for it; and if you were a regular customer and for some reason you
found yourself a centime short, then you went away empty handed.
There was no offence given, nor taken. We noticed on a few occasions
a marked difference of attitude toward the customer between America
and Paris: the customer was not treated as anything particularly special
in Paris, even with a big ticket item like buying a car; if the customer
didn't appreciate the service then he was free to go somewhere else. The
boucherie was more in tune with the customer. It was run by a huge
jocular man who sold choice meats, and whose buxom wife sported a
large mop of henna rinsed hair. She was always pleasant as she sat on a
stool beside the cash register, ostensibly to collect the money, but it was
widely believed in the *quartier* that it was to keep an eye on him because
he had quite a following among the ladies. *Le Libraire* was somewhat
forbidding: every day I would pick up the International Herald Tribune
and *Le Figaro* on my way to the *boulangérie* ---I never saw that woman's
face crack into a smile in the five years we were there. The reverse was

true at *Les Plats de Jour* , whose owners lived in our building. They were kindness itself. Unlike America, our dog was welcomed into the store as an honored guest, and treated to a choice piece of ham cut off the bone especially for her. In the village of *Auteuil,* about half a mile away, there were decidedly upscale *Charcuteries,* including *La Nôtre* whose fame was Paris wide. Whereas *les plats de jour* offered an excellent array of food designed to save you cooking the evening meal, the charcuteries specialized in presenting ready made foods as mouth watering art forms with intricate decorations. Helga soon found that while adjustments would certainly have to be made, the prospects for domestic living were on the whole good and her survey of the battlefield was not dissuading her from coming.

The transit system in Paris is quite exceptional; no spot in Paris is further than five hundred metres from a Metro stop. The ten or more lines are not color coded as in Washington, nor do they have names as in London or Tokyo, and one has to know the final destination at each end of each line in order to identify the line you want to take, such as *"Direction Porte St. Cloud".* When you have done this, you are all set, but it takes a while. Transfer directions to go from one line to another where they intersect are denoted by signs saying *"Correspondence",* which throws one at first. So Helga set about learning these mysteries, and passed her *épreuve* to gain her Tenderfoot Badge by being unceremoniously dumped to see the Impressionists at the *Jeu de Pomme* at the *Place de la Concorde,* and asked to find her own way back to the apartment in due course. She recalls that triumph in her diary, but was not so fortunate apparently in mastering the busses first time. The PC passed the apartment and also the OECD at *Porte be la Muette.* She failed to press the button so that she could get off, and was carried on to the next stop despite pleas to the driver. At that stop she was roundly cussed out by three women when she mistakenly attempted to exit by the front door instead of the center one. She arrived at the OECD for lunch, and got to know where the pennies to live on would come from. The next stop was to visit the Rothschild Bank, where we changed my account to read "M. Eric Willis et/ou Mme Helga Mancy". No one bats an eyelid at doing this in Paris, but one might hesitate to do the same here. Helga got to know the inscrutable procedures of the French

Banking system, and now had her own money shop. We were very proud of those checks – collectors items now !

The weather showed a few touches of blue sky, so we took off for Versailles and Fontainblau on the first Sunday. It was a good thing we did, for the window of opportunity closed almost immediately. The weather became even worse, cold, clammy and windy. Jack Vanderyn, who had bee instrumental in nominating me for the Paris position, was in town on business and I thought it might be appropriate to show our appreciation by offering a little hospitality as a couple for the first time. It was a bit rough on Helga in that little kitchen, but she predictably made the most of it. There were eight to dinner, and she served a superb beef stroganoff. Except when I did the cooking, tacos had been the highpoint of my previous spousal culinary experience , and this was haute cuisine indeed. I figured I could get used to that level of cooking, and my spirits rose to new highs. But the cold was getting to Helga, and she developed the inevitable sneezles and wheezles. The poor woman spent the next day in bed, and I rushed back from a lunch time trip to Printemps where I had bought a very efficient electric blower heater. It managed to take the chill off the place but no real warmth. She was determined to get up on the Saturday, her last full day, and we made our pilgrimage to Notre Dame. It was with a heavy heart on both our parts that we said goodbye at Charles de Gaulle Airport with the warm feeling that at least we should be meeting again in Washington in December. My Mother had enthusiastically agreed to come too, so we would be having the first of what proved to be many wonderful Christmases together.

11. Inside the Goldfish Bowl........ The IEA

What makes an international organization tick? What is it like inside? Although I was no stranger to dealing with foreign governments, this was my first experience of being actually part of an international organization, and being in fact an international civil servant. What did that mean, and how would I deal with that ? Would the place be rife with conflicts of interest? The simple answer is no, with very few exceptions some of which were to prove quite amusing

Although I was American, in theory one submerges that fact and transfers one's loyalty and energies to the Governing Board of the organization, in this case the International Energy Agency, and its appointed Executive Director. Thus any "directives" from home base are to be politely resisted, and the policies of international consensus pursued. This is not a happy notion to some home based bureaucrats who tended to regard you as "their boy" to whom they, through their own personal generosity, had bestowed a protracted vacation. One such instance was so gauche as to be not only counterproductive, but funny into the bargain. On this occasion I was given a very long lecture via transatlantic telephone by a former colleague on the subject of patriotism. He was a man of small stature with a sense of humor to match, so he also had the unfortunate habit of not wasting ten words when a hundred and fifty would suffice. He would talk interminably.

Since I had some other Americans in the room with me at the time, we could not resist the temptation to pass the phone around for all to benefit from his inscrutable wisdom -- if he had but known ! Although this was a trivial incident, it did highlight the inherent pressures which all the IEA staff are subject to from time to time. Representatives from home base sometimes assumed that their nominees to the IEA Staff were merely there to execute their bidding, regardless of whether the proposed course of action was in line with agreed upon international policies.

In my opinion, the tone is set by the head of the Organization. Fortunately, the Executive Director, Ulf Lantzke, was an experienced hand in the international arena and was as shrewd an individual as one could meet. He would listen with extreme courtesy and patience to a national representative pushing for a favor while calmly puffing smoke from one of his vile cheroots. He would then politely remind them of some Governing Board decisions to which they had been a party, or the wording of an Implementing Agreement between countries which their country had signed, that prevented him from acquiescing to their otherwise compelling request. He sometimes presented a disarmingly disheveled appearance but he had a way of deflecting challenges firmly without confrontation or causing offence. He was also a master of achieving consensus where non was apparent at the outset. He would seize upon some small point, reach agreement on it, and by a flicker of his eyebrow extrapolate this minor agreement to a wider consensus – an impressive performance.

There are always some jokers in the pack among visiting political appointees from Washington who lack a vestige of international savvy; the poor fellows were doomed to be ineffective from the outset. They seemed almost obsessed with the thought of Americans on the IEA staff "going native", and giving the "store away". Far from influencing the course of events, they achieved little but polite rebuffs, sometimes without their even noticing. One Assistant Secretary gathered the American members of the IEA staff together in the US Mission to the OECD, and included in his pep talk on patriotism the admonition not to read the International Herald Tribune because it was a seditious rag.

He "resigned" within the week. Another earnest but aesthetic individual eschewed Governing Board dinners held the evening before a plenary session as being somehow decadent, and an inefficient use of his time; he was totally unaware when he appeared at the Plenary Session that all the crucial deals, so necessary to success in international affairs, had been cut at that very same dinner he had chosen to miss the previous evening. He was puzzled and at the same time frustrated by the lack of response to an erudite presentation he had just made because there was no decision left to make---they had already been taken. He too lasted only a very short time.

By sharp contrast, there were US representatives both to the OECD and the IEA who commanded the highest respect for their hard work, integrity and their ability to achieve their objectives through reason and persuasion. They were stalwarts: they made serious positive contributions. Three of these people deserve particular mention. Dr Kenneth Davis was Deputy Secretary of Energy at the US Department of Energy, who devoted much time and energy to our Fusion Materials Irradiation Test Facility Project. The second was Dr. Alvin Trivelpiece, who contributed much by his presence and his solid scientific background at the Committee for Research and Development. The third is my good friend Don Kerr, then Director of Los Alamos National Laboratory, who although he could run technical rings around most of the delegates to the CRD, never deviated from being an impartial Chairman. His scientific stature, recognized by all, managed to bring meetings to definitive conclusions without trampling on any sensitivities nor causing offence to any one.

The quality of the IEA staff was of a generally very high order, as was their dedication to its success. Although it is a cynical thing to do, there was an unfortunate tendency on the part of some countries to try to "unload" some of their weaker brethren into convenient international slots, but fortunately they were few. Ulf Lantzke was well aware of these tricks, and was a man who could not be "lent on". He maintained an admirable control over the recruitment process, and resisting most attempts to dilute the professional acumen of his Agency, although he did not claim a hundred per cent infallibility. He also knew when it was time to "fold", but he always extracted a price for doing so.

The Directors, as a group, would have done credit to any organization of note, and all had distinguished careers before and after their service in the Agency. But it is the solid professional performers in the middle ranks that I would be remiss not to mention at this juncture. It is a source of enormous pleasure to Helga and me that many of the friends we made from among those younger people are still close friends today, albeit graying, twenty or more years later. It has been a source of great pride to see them excel and prosper in their subsequent careers, and to see their families grow from babies to be Graduates with Honors from Universities such as Princeton. There is still a flourishing IEA alumni Group in Washington, whose friendship continues to enrich our lives. Helga and I count this as a special gift of our days in Paris.

Concerning working with a multinational staff, I experienced no trouble whatsoever in working relationships based on national origin, nor were there any such "groupings" in the agency as a whole. I was pleasantly surprised by this, but in part it was yet another instance of the tone being set at the top of the Agency. Friendships made across national lines proved extremely durable, and as noted above, they are still strong today. Parties among the alumni group are often held in honor of overseas IEA friends who happen to be visiting Washington

The OECD has a high reputation for conducting penetrating studies across a broad spectrum of international concerns, from taxation to the environment. The plenary sessions were held in *les salles de réunions* , where simultaneous interpretation was available in a variety of languages. I am constantly amazed at the skill of these interpreters, who seem to find the right word in almost real time. When I was on the Senior Staff Board of the OECD, I came to realize the pressures on these people. Despite their crucial role in the organization, they were essentially voyeurs, contributing nothing of their own to the substance of the proceedings save their skill in translating. As a result it was my observation that they tended to become somewhat discontented with their own lives, and gravitated to other activities in the organization such as strong union participation. In this they were often effective advocates in front of the Senior Staff Board when some individual was under threat of dismissal for non performance. My tenure on this Board gave me a better appreciation of what it is like to be a long term career international civil servant bound by rigid, initiative busting, staff rules and promotion prospects, and the sometimes arbitrary salary scales often imposed thoughtlessly by representatives of member countries.

The Deputy Executive Director was Wally Hopkins. He was a bluff Yale lawyer in the true sense of the word – blunt, frank and hearty, and had been in the US Navy. He was somewhat brusque with staff members, as several of his assistants would willingly attest, but the man was kindness itself. I got to be friends with him in a strange way. He had been giving the IEA Counsel, who had also been in the US Navy, a hard time as I entered the room, and Wally conclude his harangue with the words"..... and that is how we run the ship in our Navy, Counselor". The Counselor left the room somewhat sheepishly and Wally, still a bit on fire, turned to me and said, " And how did they run the ship in your Navy, Dr Willis"? He knew I had been in the Royal Navy, and was not shy in having a dig on that account. I replied, "Well Wally, in my Navy we always contrived to have the sharp end pointing forward. We found it went much better that way". Wally went red, banged his fist on a closet door, opened it, poured me a good scotch, sat back in his easy chair, and roared with laughter. That was the beginning of a great friendship, cut short by his untimely death at aged fifty five. Despite his forbidding manner sometimes, Wally was not only a loyal deputy to Ulf Lantzke, but a true professional when it came to drafting sensitive communiques after Governing Board Meetings. He could think clearly under intense pressure, working though the night if need be, and would come up with precisely the right wording, terse and tight, to satisfy all the participants by the next morning. It was a rare gift.

On the social side, Wally could admittedly get a little animated at parties, and Helga too had a few run-ins with him. One day Don Kerr said to her, "Now Helga, just remember he's a Yaley". Helga was not sure quite what was meant by this, but when she did bear that in mind, they too became the best of friends. Wally and I would often frequent the Stella Brasserie in Rue Victor Hugo, where the oysters were just about the best I ever had. I had never felt partial to oysters prior to coming to Paris, but Wally made a convert of me. Today, I can never pass up a chance to get some, but they never come up to Stella Brasserie standards.

There were just a few treasured perks that appeared to come with the job at the OECD. One such was the ability to buy gasolene coupons free of French tax – an enormous boon. Another was a duty free liquor and wine allowance, which permitted one to be fairly generous at home receptions. Yet another was an in house garage which permitted one to have your car serviced during the day---what a blessing that mechanic was. The OECD had a small commissary store where one could buy choice cheeses, meats, and other groceries. I am told that the forces of the ungodly have since withdrawn these and other privileges in the name of egalitarianism, not to mention penny pinching. In my time there, I have to concede that they did serve to put a little frosting on the cake.

Some of the member country attendees at IEA General Board Meetings seemed be a little larger than life, and were given nick-names appropriate to their style. The Austrian Ambassador was infatuated with his own importance, and was given the nick-name of Count Pumpernickel. He would strut into a meeting when it was well underway, ostentatiously tap his stand-in underling on the shoulder so that he could take his place, and generally make his arrival known to all present. Likewise the ubiquitous and somewhat pushy Italian Ambassador was referred to as Signor So-So. There was also a staff member who Wally once upbraided for reading the newspaper with his feet on his desk at 10am. He came to my office to bitterly protest. "…. but it is my job to read my paper before I go to lunch" was his plaintive excuse. He was so insensitive to everything and everybody that he somehow acquired the honorary title of Baron von Pick-Helmet. It is just possible that he was among those lesser achievers who some governments were inclined to "dump" on the Agency by default. It was a cynical way of doing things but,. regretfully, it happened once in a while

   In summary, my experience of the IEA attests to the strength of its people -- people who believed in what they were doing and gave of their best. The "walk-on" characters provide light relief, to be sure, but in no way detracted from the great service which was rendered to the International Community by the professional staff in the wake of the Oil Crisis of the Seventies by first rate individuals, senior and junior. It was a privilege to have been counted among them.

12. Bread and Butter

If the quality of the mid level professionals was of a very high order, then so were the responsibilities they were asked to undertake. Although the issues were complex and the canvas broad, a few minutes to capture that fascinating picture might assure the reader that despite the obvious attractions of Paris as a place to live, work was not only a serious business but an absorbing and rewarding one as well.

I have dealt earlier (Chapter 6) with certain policy initiatives which had been undertaken, namely the Strategic Review to chart a course for IEA Energy R&D, and the High Level Group on major Commercialization initiatives. The main thrust of the Office was however the encouragement of vigorous energy research programs within member countries, and at the same time to foster international co-operation in that research where appropriate. This could be termed the "Bread and Butter" work.

The encouragement of domestic research within each of the member countries was embodied in the Country Review Series. Every year, a number of countries submitted themselves to a review of their programs by representatives of other member countries. This was a serious and time consuming effort, involving on-site visits and a review of both programs and the budgeted funds allocated to them. There was a companion review series on broader energy policies also undertaken under IEA auspices and conducted by the so-called Long

Term Office. Often, the results of the review were used by researchers as a club to beat on country governments for increased funding for their programs, but that was not the prime aim of the exercise ! I participated in such a review of Japan, and I was most impressed by the openness of such a major country to the process. The amount one learned about the way other countries organized their government decision making processes was most revealing. They varied widely. In the USA, I was familiar with the Departmental budgeting process followed by the Congressional Authorization of programs and the Appropriation of funds. "Authorization" is like opening a bank account and "Appropriation" is like putting funds into the account on which to write checks. The Japanese relied heavily on the consensus process for developing programs, which were submitted to the "Diet" (the Japanese Parliament) for approval. In Britain, where the Cabinet ministers are also Members of Parliament, the budgetary process is less confrontational in Parliament---the Treasury has a big say ! In smaller Switzerland, measures often are stalled because in many unexpected instances, such as some conservation measures, each of the Cantons has to be not only consulted but a vote taken. The Review process was successful because it depended upon the consent of the reviewed. Each year, the results of the reviews conducted that year were published in full, and the results presented to the whole Committee for Research and Development.

The cooperation in individual international energy research projects was heavily dependent upon the involvement of the United States. As we have seen, the US had already embarked on a major investment in energy research, and other countries, with less resources available to them were looking for leadership in this new field. The mechanism for establishing a project was the "Implementing Agreement". The IEA was in a sense the catalyst in the process, providing the international umbrella under which the project was undertaken and the legal framework uniting the parties to contribute towards a common goal. Once formed, a project under an Implementing Agreement was autonomous, having its own executive committee and management to supervise the budget and ensuring the appropriate results. The executive committees were required to submit progress reports to the

CRD. The level of national investments in energy R&D peaked about 1980 and declined by 1985 when it became clear that the oil price had substantially declined.

There were four research sectors established, each with a Working Group derived from member countries to supervise and coordinate the sectoral activities. The secretariat was an ex-officio member of the Working Groups on behalf of the Committee for Research and Development (CRD). The four energy sectors embraced:

Energy End-Use Technologies (Conservation)
Fossil Fuel Technology
Renewable Energy
and, Controlled Thermonuclear Fusion

The very broad spectrum of scientific disciplines required the most technically qualified people to staff the Office. Each Staff member was assigned to oversee the activities of one sector, and we were fortunate enough to attract people of different nationalities who were up to the task. The great joy of being involved in such a wide ranging program was that one was always learning something new, while at the same time working in an international dimension which sometimes challenged more than just one's scientific acumen !

13. Almost like feeling at "home".

Subsequent to Helga's departure, and as November came upon us, the weather started its dreary descent into winter drabness. The sun apparently goes to sleep about that time, and is not to be disturbed before March. I was pretty much used to this because of my London background, but it was nonetheless disconcerting to witness it once more. The days were short and gray, and the morning conversation in the elevator on the way out to the street echoed a daily dismal theme.:

"C'est triste, n'est-ce pas?"...*"Oui!"*
"C'est lourde aussi!"...*"Oui, c'est dommage"*
"Il fait des nuages"... *"C'est vrai"*
"C'est brumeux", ...*"Bien sûr"*
"Le temps fait orageux"...*"Oh-la-la"*
"It fait du brouillard" ....*"Ah, mais oui"*
"Il pleut, je crois"...*"Oui, mais c'est normale, ça"*

These scintillating observations, and the almost monosyllabic responses, were exchanged with mindless resignation: they expressed neither the hope nor the expectation that the weather might clear up during the day. The Paris weather is in marked contrast with home in Washington, which one forgets is at about the same latitude as Tunis. While not immune from its gray days, when there are sunny periods the sun is higher in the sky, and the sunshine has a welcome warming effect on both body and soul. In Northern Europe, the sun is lower in the sky, and when it does shine in Winter it does so through a watery haze like a pale yellow soup plate. The otherwise admirable Metro responds to the weather by providing an incubation system second to none — if there is a newly arrived bug from sunnier climes in the Mediterranean, Mother Metro treasures the new organism with maternal care. It has a dissemination mechanism which would be the envy of a terrorist in biological warfare, and within days the population is nursing juicy respiratory infections generically classified as "*La Rhume*" or "*La Grippe*", a Cold or the 'Flu respectively. The doctors diagnose it as the Paris Crud, and treat it with the stock remedy of two aspirins, plenty of rest, and lots of fluids !

I was beginning to get a little more venturesome in the entertainment arena. In this regard the charcuteries were a godsend, allowing one to pass off delectable gourmet items without so much as a blush. The Committee for Research and Development had its first meeting after Tokyo in early December, and the delegates would be coming to town. I met Don Kerr, the Chairman, off the train from Brussels at the *Gare du Nord*, and took him home to stay for the first of many pleasant subsequent visits to our apartment. We had both received much hospitality from the Boxers, and we felt it was high time to reciprocate. We invited Leslie and Colette Boxer to have dinner with us, and the two temporary bachelors were afraid they might disgrace themselves with their cuisine. I remember we managed a presentable fish dish, but when it came to the dessert we agonized mightily. We wanted to make a chocolate mousse sauce with pears, and all we could think of were Mars Bars as the main ingredient. The melting bars merely produced a lumpy gooey sticky mess in the pan, and there was no hint of a mousse. Almost in an act of desperation we sloshed a big slug of brandy into it. The mess bubbled and frothed mightily, and we were afraid of the most dire consequences. To our utter amazement, the result was the smoothest creamy mousse we could ever have wished for. Our guests were duly impressed, as indeed we were, and asked for the recipe. But we were too embarrassed to reveal that the "treat" was in fact nothing more than regular Mars Bars, and said that we would provide a copy of the recipe when it was time for them to leave. I am not sure to this day if we gave any unintended offence, but we sheepishly handed each of them a Mars Bar in its wrapper as they went out the door.

I had a welcome mission in November: Canada is always an attractive country to visit, and particularly, in winter. While we were in Hong Kong, Peter Dyne had suggested that he would like me to meet his Energy Staff in Ottawa and, since Canada was an enthusiastic member of the IEA I was more than happy to make the visit. Ottawa had developed beyond belief from the time I had first visited it in 1956. At that time it was still a primitive town, hardly a city, and I remember being shocked that this was the capital city of Canada. The first part of the road in from the rudimentary Newlands Airport was still unpaved. A block away from Constitution Square, aptly called Confusion Square by the natives, the buildings were drab and nondescript. Trams threaded their way lugubriously through the town, and a plethora of wires dangled everywhere like a giant cobweb. Nearly twenty five years later it had been transformed into a well designed and bustling center, with bright new buildings and fine archetecture. The old railroad, which had gone straight through the city center, had been rerouted around the city and the old majestic Union Station was a refurbished civic center. Canadians adapt to their climate with a certain relish. It was a harsh winter already, but the Rideau Canal serves as a built in skating rink, and was already in full use. It was my Birthday that day, and I felt a certain jollity in revisiting an old friend.

Meanwhile, back "home" in Paris, the OECD was celebrating it twentieth anniversary of its founding in 1960. I have an imposing bronze medallion in my study to commemorate the twentieth anniversary of the OECD which had been founded in 1960. There was an impressive ceremony which featured no less than the President of the *Republique de France, Giscard d'Estaing. D'Estaing* was often criticized in the media for the regal style of his Presidency, and he appropriately gave the commemoration address sitting in a Louis XIV style gilt chair. It was fascinating to hear this man speak in person, for he is an extremely eloquent speaker, with that cultured french cadence which makes the most mundane statement sound like poetry. I have to say that I personally was, and remain, fascinated by the man. A year or so later

Helga and I were to nearly bump into him when hauling our luggaga from the car park at *Orly-Ouest* Airport – even in those circumstances, he was charm itself. It was a great pity that he failed to get reelected the following year, but he made a fatal mistake when debating his equally well spoken opponent, *François Mitterand,* on television just before the election. He talked down from a great height to his opponent on the subject of foreign affairs, and Mitterand cut him short quipping, "*Monsieur, je ne suis pas votre élève*" ! It was a brilliant move, for the wording is interesting. In America all persons in an educational status are students. In Europe "students" are only those attending universities, while those still in grade and high schools are termed "pupils". *Élève* is a pupil and, beside the force of the put down, that made *d'Estaing* out to be merely a preachy schoolmaster. We groaned as we watched, for it had a chilling and lasting effect – the contest was over.

During this period, I usually had lunch in the building. The OECD had three separate eating facilities on the top floor. It had an adequate snack bar, which did good omelettes and salads but the formidable help were terminally miserable. Then there was the Cafeteria, tersely known as the "Self", which contradicted all the marvelous things you have ever heard about french cuisine, and it is doubtful if it will be ever written up in the "Guide Michelin". The diplomats and senior staff had access to the restaurant, where one had table cloths and wine glasses, and it has to be said that the food was quite good. One usually used this quick entertaining when one was rushed, and could not afford the two hours it took to go to a nearby lunch place. Lunches in the local watering holes are where much delicate business was conducted, or so it is alleged. Paris lunches are an institution – a bottle of wine between two is standard ration, and the food is usually excellent. There is no apparent rush to get back to the office, for indeed this is where the work is. Delegations used the opportunity to entertain senior staff and other delegations, not to mention themselves indulging in a first rate free meal. That is with the honorable exception of the US Delegation who dodged this trap, not for any high minded altruistic reason, but simply that they never had any representation funds.

Eric H. Willis

There are three distinct levels of eating out in Paris, each with its own character and charm. At the lowest level, but not to be sniffed at, is the side walk café. The food is basic, as is the ambiance, but a *"jambon sandwich au beurre"* washed down with a jar of *Kronenburg 66* is magnificent in its own right. Next up are the Brasseries. It is thought that the waiters at Brasseries go to a special school to perfect their sassiness; foreigners attribute rudeness to this art form, but in fact they are just acting out the part that is expected of them and for which they have laboriously trained. When they studiously ignore you for more important things, and one calls out to them, they invariably reply *"J'arrive"* which roughly translated means "Belt up. I'll come in my own good time". Brasseries serve very good food of the steak and *casserolée* variety, and the house wine is usually superior to many of chateau origin. It is not uncommon to see, on the way out, waiters pouring unfinished wine into new bottles to be sold again later. An oyster stand outside the entrance is often a clear indication of Brasserie status, and the "oyster shucker" is there in all weathers. Restaurants range from the barely affordable up to the stratospheric. Those ,with varying degrees of success, carry the banner of haute cuisine. Almost invariably they are quite excellent, and tend to be pricier than the brasseries. Michelin Stars are coveted, and the cost that goes with the rank of "Three Stars" ensures either an "expense account only" clientele or foreigners on a binge. Everyone cultivates his favorite hideout, and invariably frequents it regularly. We had one next to the apartment which was acceptable, but when the old curmudgeon who was the owner died, it was taken over by a young and very talented chef called "Patricke". When I visited the same restaurant fifteen years later, my credit card took an awful whack – but the meal was quite memorable. Actually, that is not quite true – I cannot remember the meal, but I do remember the tab.

Preparations for Helga to come to Paris had to include one critical factor: the consent of the French Government ! Essentially I was proposing to bring in an illegal immigrant because she would be living in Paris outside the normal permitted stay of a visitor. There is a way around this which entailed getting a *Certificat d'Aubergement,* which in effect would say that Helga could neither work nor ever be a charge on French public funds. Paris is divided up for administrative purposes into *Arondissments.* This certificate was obtainable, it was thought, at the *Marie* of the local *Arondissment,* the 16th. The Marie is the administrative building which among other things performs weddings. Leslie Boxer and I tootled down to *Avenue Henri Martin* full of anticipation that soon we would have this little problem under control. Oh dear no! One could not get the certificate without the person actually present because of all the particulars required, and one could not get the person into the country without it. Catch 22 ! I was told that one had to start with the French Embassy in Washington with Helga in tow, which we later did, only for them to pass the buck back to Paris. Arriving in Paris in January, we duly tried to get the certificate at the *Prefecture de Police on Quai du Marché Neue* in the company of a motley collection of would-be au pairs. Despite what passed for conversations with disinterested *functionaires* all was to no avail, even with Helga now inside the country. So Helga lived in Paris eventually on a tourist visa, and we went in and out of the country often enough to perpetuate that status until such time as we made the lady "legal". eight months later. Then she was accorded diplomatic status, as was I. As for Americans getting married in France – no way! Everything short of the Bible would have to be translated into French, and notarized. But that's a story for later !

Christmas was on the way, so I visited Printemps to see what I could pick up in the way of Christmas decorations. Christmas in France is on a much lower key than in either America, Germany, or England. *Père Noël* was there to be sure, but not the omnipresent figure one finds in America. Christmas Cards are virtually unheard of, and any cards that are available combine *Joyeux Noël* with *Bonne Nouvelle Anneé,* greetings for the New Year. Christmas trees were not in evidence, and there is no equivalent to the splendid German tradition of the *Kristkindelmarkt* where there are ornaments in profusion in a colorful display in outdoor markets. I felt this was all somehow rather cheerless, and a bit of a let down. I managed to rummage through a few trays to find one or two ornaments, but that was it. I dutifully hung them up in the Living Room when I got home, so as not to have to look at the Calendar to remind me that Christmas was on the way.

The Office duly had a Christmas Party as a prelude to the coming holiday, and I think Niels de Terra must have had a hand in this since he lived on the *Ile Saint Louis*. At *41 Rue Saint Louis en L'Ile,* the main street, there is a place which is almost a legend called the *Le Sergent Recruteur.* It is ostentatiously primitive, has bare scrubbed wooden tables, and is lit by candles stuck into wine bottles with the drippings of the previous twenty candles adorning the bottle. The menu is fixed: a wide variety of breads and sausages are served in baskets. The main dish is tasty plain fare, but since the wine flows freely gourmet offerings would have been wasted After the initial shock, every one is guaranteed a fine evening out !

Ah, yes. I was " almost at home" here. All I needed now was my Helga

14. The first Christmas in Arlington

My Mother arrived in Paris from England for a few days in advance of when we were to fly to the States to spend Christmas with Helga. It was to be a family occasion, with all the Children, a Grandchild, plus our two Mothers. This was a vote of confidence, if ever there was one, on the part of the family concerning the future prospects for Helga and Eric. The goodwill was as extraordinary as it was encouraging, and Helga and I were resolved to repay their confidence in the years ahead.

In winter, TWA made landfall in the US at Boston. There, we cleared customs and took a second plane into Washington National. Helga was there to welcome us with her usual warm smile. That was about the only thing that was warm that evening, for our first reaction on going to the car was – grrhh ! It's cold ! The cold seemed to strip you naked and bite into your bones. It was destined to get colder as the holidays progressed, and poor Win didn't have this in mind when she had packed. But the warmth of being together again was to more than make up for this inconvenience.

At this point I would like to introduce Monika.. Monika is Helga's only child, and I am happy to say that she now has been my own only daughter for many happy years now. We had to break new ground in the State of Virginia to adopt an adult instead of a kiddy-winky. At the time however, I was "Mum's" new boy friend and for a variety of reasons somewhat suspect. To say that she had a jaundiced view of Helga's previous spouse would be an understatement, as indeed to some extent Nigel had of mine. Son Martin was married, and lived in Ohio, so although he was involved he was less intimately so. Nevertheless, the three adult children had to be persuaded that this time around things might be different. Helga and I were painfully aware that only time, not words, would do the convincing so we had to set our sights on the long haul. Twenty or more years later, "Mum" and "Dad" feel they have given of their best, and hope they have passed the test, but who are we to say ?

Helga had arranged a party on the 23rd, and it was quite an affair. This was in a sense our coming out party, and our respective friends were able to get used to the idea that Helga and I were serious about the future. Helga had resigned from the Civil Service earlier in the month: this was a momentous move -- people with twenty or more years of service and the rank of GS-15 simply do NOT do that. The fact that she was planning to join me in Paris in three short weeks really caught their attention. Many admired the way she was prepared to go plunging into uncharted waters, but at the same time they may have feared for her burning too many bridges at one time. Since I was going to be the recipient of this act of faith, I was deeply conscious of both the honor this bestowed upon me and the nature of the responsibility I was happy to undertake. The people present seemed to be aware of such undercurrents behind this party, but whatever their reservations might have been in private they were hugely supportive in public. Maybe it was a case of their praying that "Fortune would favor the Brave !

The house sported a fine Christmas Tree, with presents in profusion under it. You may ask how I remember such thine – the answer is simple; I have a photograph of it right in front to of me. This is the period when we started to collect a photographic record of our adventures, and there are now some thirty volumes in the library. We often said that since we were getting together later in life than most, we did not have enough of the "Do You Remember Whens?" that folks of marital longevity usually share. This point was vividly, but sadly, brought home to us recently when we saw an interview with Nancy Reagan concerning her husband's battle with Alzheimer's Disease. She said, " The Golden Years are when you can sit back, hopefully, and exchange memories. And that is the worst part of the disease – there's nobody to exchange memories with – and we had a lot of memories. There were times when I had to catch myself because I'd reach out and start to say, ' Honey, <u>remember when</u> ....?' " We now are blessed with so many of these "remember when's" stacked away that we are starting to forget the chronology, let alone the details. The library helps jog the memories of the now feeble minded who, on rushing downstairs to get something important, cannot remember what it was when they reach the bottom !

Helga had two dogs at the time. One was an Australian Terrier named "Krümmel", which I am told is German for crumbs. Krümmel was an endearing pint sized little animal, with a vivacious personality. Unfortunately, Krümmel was fourteen and with a heart murmur, so we were advised that she would have a hard time with the trip. Happily, Monika agreed to take her, and we regretfully left her behind. The second dog was "Putzi", whose name means something like being "cute". She was five, so she was quite young enough for the trip, and subsequent Parisian life. She was a long haired dachshund, and a beautiful specimen; heads would turn to look at her as she "sacheted" along the *trottoir* with us in tow. She became a well known figure around the *Quartier* in Paris, and was welcomed everywhere – waiters would open restaurant doors with the welcome "Bon Soir, Madmoiselle Putzi". If this was a case of "Love me, love my dog", I was an easy push over. Putzi and I had a love affair of our own, only broken when she died in my arms ten years later. So began my devotion to long haired dachshunds, and there has been no competition from other brands since. Period.

Christmas Dinner was the first gathering of what was to be our new family. There were six of us. Helga and I; our two Mothers, Hertha and Win; and two children, Monika and Nigel. We have had bigger and more elaborate Christmas Dinners since that time (the record is fourteen people), but this one has to be the most significant. Son Martin, his wife Debbie, and young Eric now aged four months, joined us the day after to complete the roster. What a blessing this Christmas period proved to be.

Hertha went back to her home in Florida in a few days, while the rest of us went up to the mountains to a home I had at Wintergreen. The cold weather was even colder at 3300 feet, and promised good skiing. Now a word about my skiing prowess is in order here. I had first stood on skis on these very slopes at the age of fifty, and some might say that this is too late in life to reach anything like Olympic standard: they may well have a point. Nevertheless, I felt that I was making splendid progress. After all I had managed to get down the slope to the bottom in one piece, only pausing a few times to kiss the snow. And didn't I ski sublimely passed Helga and Martin when they were both lying in the snow having wiped out? So how did I come to get the name of the "Gorilla"? The reason for this remains a mystery to me. Admittedly, I do sometimes tend to snow plough a bit when maybe I should be pirouetting with elegant tight turns – but the "Gorilla" ! Me ! Anyway, I have now retired from the sport, pleading "no contest" to the onslaughts of the berserk bowling balls who today dominate the slopes.

My Mother Win was liberal enough in her ideas, but there were some she felt were important enough to make her views known. She took me aside, and said in her sweet little way that commanded attention, "Dear, don't you think you ought to buy Helga a ring to go to Paris with ?". " Why would I do a thing like that?", I replied in all innocence. "Well Dear," she responded,"she may not be sporting a Wedding Ring yet, but she ought to be able to show people she is not foot loose and fancy free". I conceded her point; after all, I was essentially smuggling Helga into France with no visible means of support, and a ring was the least I could do. Accordingly, Helga and I trotted off to the Tiny Jewel Box, a jewelers in Connecticut Avenue which specializes in antique items of very fine quality. Twenty two years later, we are still on their mailing list, so either we made a big impression or they are eternal optimists. Maybe it was because I persuaded them to take a credit card denominated in French Francs, no small feat in those days! We selected a really lovely ring with a center sapphire surrounded by diamonds. And so it was that on New Years Eve 1980 I gave Helga a ring to signify to the world my love and commitment, and I admire it on her finger to this day !

Another purchase in Connecticut Avenue involved Stereo equipment. I had shipped my stereo set to Paris, but it neither produced good quality nor was it exactly compact. Nothing close. It was of the vintage where such installations were more to be looked at than listened to. It was a huge and elegant sideboard sized piece with great woodwork but housing electronics that could easily have been put into two shoe boxes. It was a kind of Tutankhamen Tomb wired for sound. It won't come as a surprise that it was one of the things Helga had earmarked for, shall we say euphemistically, "replacement" on her first visit to the apartment in August. Making sure of the elementary requirement that the equipment could be adapted to French voltage, we bought two speakers and an elegant rack of electronics that would have done credit to Star Wars. This was to come over in the second consignment of furniture, which the OECD generously allowed me, and which would contain some very nice pieces of Helga's. Such is the conservative nature of our electronic acquisitions that the amplifier was only finally decommissioned as an antique just last Christmas when a new generation of Star Wars II equipment finally took its place.

Finally the time came when Mother Win and I should return to Europe, and await Helga at the crack of dawn at Charles de Gaulle Airport in two weeks time, the 16th January. It would be her turn to arrive on a one way ticket; she would be arriving to a big welcome, to be sure, but there is still something compelling about that one-way ticket! It was even colder than when we had arrived in Washington, and Helga lent Mother her fur coat to travel in. It turned out to be non too much in the way of protection. When we arrived in Boston, it was so cold that the ramp was completely frozen, and all the passengers had to disembark through the rear door staircase, and cross the tarmac in the freezing cold wind. Poor Win was frozen stiff, even though she was in a wheel chair and smothered in blankets. The cold weather delayed the onward flight for a few hours, and the morning was well advanced when we eventually arrived in Paris. Unfortunately she did catch a chill, and I had to nurse her for a few days before she was fit enough to take the plane back to London Gatwick. My sister Doreen lived close by, and was able to take over Win's care. Win's advice was always considered, and given without any hint of reproach. She was not only a kind, but a gutsy woman.

And so my Bachelorhood in Paris was rapidly coming to an end after eight months. It had been quite an adventure, but I was looking forward to another chapter starting in two weeks time. The beachhead had been established – now was the time to move forward. Paris is an experience that is the better for sharing, and who better to share it with than Helga.

Part Two - The Shakedown Cruise: The Second Eight Months

15. New Beginnings.

They were not at all inviting that morning: the streets of Paris I mean. It wasn't raining for once, and for mid January it was quite mild. No, it was misty and daybreak was still two hours away as I emerged from the parking garage, and the automatic door shut firmly with a thud behind me. The mist immediately condensed on the windshield as I put on the wipers and proceeded slowly up *Boulevard Murat*. I had not gone the hundred yards to *Porte Molitor* before I saw a lone couple forlornly waiting beside the curb near the corner. There was ostensibly a taxi stand there with a phone from which taxis were to be summoned – I had yet to see any connection between the stand and a taxi, so I stopped and asked if they wanted help. At six in the morning, anyone standing on the corner obviously needed help! They said they were trying to get to Charles de Gaulle Airport, and I replied that they were in luck – jump in! I was going there too to pick up Helga off the plane from Washington!

They were foreigners in Paris, like myself, which meant we got on just fine. It is an extraordinary thing but it is much easier to converse with a stranger in French than with a Parisian in French – even though your French may be painful to their ears, the stranger makes an effort to understand you. No such concession is accorded by a Parisian. We got on to the *Périphérique*, which was blissfully empty, and quickly covered the normally significant distance to the turn off to the *Autoroute du Nord* at *Porte La Chapelle.* . Being a rail buff, I am always intrigued by bustling marshaling yards of *St. Ouen* beside the rail line out of the *Gare du Nord*; they alone seemed busy at that hour with the clatter of trains being assembled breaking the unaccustomed quietness. The drive out to Roissy was easy too, and I dropped my grateful passengers at the Arrivals Door — I had saved them a few hundred francs too, and they were kind enough to offer to pay. I declined, of course---welcome to a bit of Parisian kindness!

One privilege accorded to diplomats was free reserved parking space at the airports, and I readily took advantage of that convenient concession and made my way down to the Arrivals area. There is a small and grotty café situated alongside the Arrivals Board in the Concourse. It does a roaring trade, because the news on the Board frequently conveys lengthy waits, and lengthy waits mean endless cups of coffee. Planes arrive from all around the world, but the ones from francophone countries in Africa invariably account for the bulk of those waiting. It was not difficult to see why. The board normally announces to the faithful how many minutes a plane is "en retard", which is usually only a minor annoyance rather than a cause for concern. However, in the case of African airlines one has to pay particular attention to see whether "en retard" means that they should have arrived sometime yesterday, or any other day. "Annulée" is another common announcement with these airlines, and one wonders whether it is worse being grounded <u>by</u> them or flying <u>with</u> them. I once flew Ethiopian Airlines -- it was a shock to discover what had happened to Pan Am's very first Boeing 707's — the original Pan Am blue had faded to obscurity, the seats were the original, and any paint had been worn bare. The toilets were, shall we say, appropriately primitive. And yes, it was predictably "en retard"!

I was here to meet TWA 890 from Washington, which was posted as *"quarante-cinq minutes en retard"*, which in the parlance of the Arrivals Board meant it was right on time. As the appointed time approached, I drank only my second coffee, paid the extortion which passed for the check, and made my leisurely way through customs to the baggage carousels. In those days security was, shall we say, relaxed and my *Carte Grise* diplomatic card allowed me in to hallowed ground with no problem. I do not think the United Sates offered reciprocal arrangements in Washington! The original terminal at Charles de Gaulle Airport had an intriguing design, and passengers are conveyed to one level from another by moving belts contained in glass tubes through which they pass like globs of food in a transparent intestine. There seemed no valid logistical reason at all why passengers should change levels in the first place, but the visual effect was striking. It also, at that time, provided a convenient way of getting into the baggage retrieving area without going through the customs doors. One first went down the Departures tube, and then following the arriving passengers back up the Arrivals tube to the baggage carousels. I can't imagine this being designed today!

In no time at all, one of these people movers disgorged Helga at Carousel 22 where I was waiting. What a wonderful moment. It was difficult to take all in, and in those prosaic surroundings, just how momentous it really was. Despite the feeling that one should retain ones's decorum in such places, there were a lot of huggings and kissings while waiting for the baggage to arrive. Putzi announced herself very vocally from her traveling kennel which arrived separately, safe and sound. She appeared not overtly any worse for the experience, which was a distinct relief. After collecting five suitcases, a trunk and a kennel, we marched off through the somnolent customs men, and up to the car park which was in the upper stories of the terminal. I drove the car out onto the highway just as dawn was breaking, and we left the Airport to begin Helga's truly first drive "home".

Since she was exhausted, both physically and mentally, I put her to bed with Putzi and I slipped out discretely to go to work. It was still only about nine o'clock! By this time, eight months into my tenure, there was plenty happening during the day, and we were about to experience a major climacteric in the energy field. In a few days we were about to have a new President inaugurated in the United States, and there were already rumblings of major changes of emphasis in energy policy. One of his campaign promises had been to abolish the Department of Energy as a first priority, so some of the senior bureaucrats committed to the old way of doing things in Washington were already proclaiming their born again persuasions. Despite their protestations of being holier than the new Pope, their pleas of innocence were to fall on deaf ears, and when new political appointees were later installed, they all got short but unlamented shrift. Suffice to say that the Department is still in place!

My "welcome aboard" dinner consisted of the largest Dover Sole I could find in the market. In fact I have never seen one that size since! I served it Meunier style on the bone, and it fileted to perfection. It was a great feeling to sit down at <u>our</u> dinner table for what was to be the first meal of all these years together. After dinner, we had to "walk" dear Putzi, who seemed already very much at home. There was no "doggy door" for her to escape into the garden to do her business, so she had to be "walked" on a regular schedule. Despite her obvious need to "go", a mile of walking produced nary a drop. When she hadn't produced a drop in the morning, we got rather anxious. Colette Boxer produced the name of a vet, and so it was that we made our first call to his"cabinet". It transpired that the poor animal had a bladder infection; when this was treated it restored her to a more reliable regime. Actually, she became a model Parisienne, and could be absolutely relied upon anywhere and anytime.

It turned out that Helga had arrived in a particularly absorbing week from the viewpoint of both my work and the IEA as an institution. I called at our local Charcuterie on the way home to bring some "goodies" for lunch, and found the new arrivals awake if not entirely rested. January 16th was a Friday, and so I had the weekend in front of me to help Helga settle in. I anticipated that it was going to be difficult for her initially. From an all consuming build-up of activity and excitement, not to mention a responsible job, she was going to discover on Monday the inevitable let-down of being in a strange environment with nothing to do. That could only be tough – there is only so much rearranging and tidying up one can do! This was going to take all the sensitivity and support I could muster, but there was no alternative but to get through the doldrums of the first weeks in order for her to have life with a purpose and not to precipitate a major disappointment. This was going to be a learning period for us both – what would the learning curve be like ?

16 ....the learning curve

Helga had spent two or three years during and after the war at a French speaking school in Switzerland, and since she has a natural flair for languages anyway she felt it was a good idea for her to bring her French up to concert pitch once more by going to school full time. Nigel had already been to the *Alliance Française*, so I knew where to find it on *Boulevard Raspail*, near *Montparnasse*. Helga duly enrolled, and was placed in a more advanced class. She threw herself into the task with her usual 110% determination, going to school in the morning, and performing the exercises at home in the afternoon. She became one of the legions of Paris Commuters each morning on Ligne 10 which wended its way from Auteuil across the 15th Arrondissment to *Sèvres Babylon*, and there changed to alight at *Notre Dame des Champs* near the Alliance. Her fellow students were a motley collection, mostly from francophone countries and from all walks of life. Many were "au pair" girls and Helga was easily the oldest in the class. She rapidly became the "Mother Superior" to the younger students, including the occasional confessional! French was taught in a no-nonsense orthodox fashion, but the interaction with this cross section of society also introduced Helga to a lexicon not found in Larousse Dictionaries; a mastery of this *patois* came in very handy when she had to deal with stall holders in the market or cashiers at the *Euromarché*. Helga absorbs language easily, but it has to be said that the *Alliance* made her work at it, and she responded. This was no push over.

Bit by bit, Helga gained her own footing in her new environment. The second shipment of household goods, in effect Helga's consignment, arrived in record time early in February. This included a Persian carpet which replaced the large machine made one that I had brought over, and which was consigned to the *"Cave"* for the duration. There was also a bright red Korean cutlery chest which we put in the hallway to make a cheery impression as one entered the apartment. The silver cutlery was a welcome addition because we now had elegant place settings. Her beautiful Imari set of plates and dishes ensured that we would no longer have to rush into the kitchen to wash dishes half way through a meal. The leavening of the erstwhile bachelor apartment with Helga's bits and pieces soon gave it a new "air", and the scene was set to buy new items which would be the first approach to a joint venture. The first item was the purchase of light fixtures to fix on to the bare wires which protruded from the walls at strategic spots. We resorted to *Au Bon Marché* rather than pricey boutiques, and even there we had sticker shock. It was not so much the price of each item, which was bad enough, but when you have to outfit the whole apartment at once with light fixtures the cost soon mounts up.

It was while sitting at the top of a step ladder trying to install one of the wretched fittings on the wall that I pulled a fast one which nearly had Helga apoplectic. She called out with some clever witticism from the kitchen, to which I replied "That sounds like a typical Little Woman remark". There was a deathly silence, as I glanced at the second hand of my watch. Then the eruption occurred – Helga came storming out of the kitchen with a "What the.............!!!!!" and a face to match. I looked up from my watch, and said with a grin, " Heavens, I thought you would never come. It took you eleven seconds !!" We had a good laugh, and it has been a household joke ever since. Provided I don't call her the Little Woman, that is !

The apartment had no drapes or curtains of any sort -- neither were there valances or curtain rods. It was like furnishing a new house. We were high enough up that no one could see in, but the windows were large and looked very bare. Again resorting to *Au Bon Marché*, we ordered some curtains with a loose weave. We have them in our home at Wintergreen to this day, so they have lasted!. Our French was still "raw", so there was much gesticulation with the salesperson to pass on the measurements, and in due course the curtains arrived. The top was gathered in a way we had not come across before. There were strings attached to it which seemed to serve no apparent reason – so Helga saw fit to cut them off, only to find that the strings were there for a purpose after all. By adjusting the strings one could adjust the curtains to fit whatever size of window one wanted. How one learn's things in a foreign land!

My sofa and easy chairs had been recovered by a "previous regime", and understandably did nor fit into Helga's scheme of things. I certainly agreed, although the furniture itself was really of excellent quality and merited recovering. Helga had spotted a diminutive storefront down Boulevard Murat which contained an upholsterers workshop. She chatted him up in her usual way, and selected some material which promised to be durable enough. He and a helper arrived at the apartment and duly carried the sofa and chairs down the ten flights of stairs since there was no way they were going to fit in the diminutive elevator. In a very long due course, and many thousands of francs later, our living room was restored to the point where we could receive guests. The job was exceedingly well done, and added much to our decor. But I gulped when I saw the bill, so it was another lesson for us about doing business in France – things were going to cost an arm and a leg!

It seemed that being "á deux" at last was the key to invitations to dinner parties. Or maybe it was because Helga's magnetic personality outweighed my more formaldemeanor. Whatever the reason, we started getting invitations as soon as she appeared on the scene. There are some interesting differences in entertaining between the two continents. Gastric juices, it would appear, work on a different time schedule and are asked to digest totally different foods. Whereas in America, one might arrive at six-thirty for a seven o'clock dinner leaving at nine thirty to ten, in Paris one arrives at eight for dinner at nine and departure not before midnight. Dinners in the US are extremely pleasant occasions, to be sure, but in Paris they are elevated to the level of serious events conceived to savor the cuisine, admire the table decoration, drool over the paintings, flatter the hostess, eulogize the wine, and test the mettle of your fellow guests.

An adequate arrival period is an hour to accommodate stragglers. It is considered impolite to arrive at the appointed time, which is adhered to only by Americans, Scandinavians and Germans who dutifully appear on your doorstep one minute after the appointed hour. A quarter of an hour late is normal, a half hour is acceptable, three quarters of an hour is not considered rude, but an hour is pushing it. However, arriving after the principal guest has arrived is not considered good form. That worthy never arrives early, because that defeats the whole purpose of his entering center stage to receive the conclave of accolades from lesser mortals.

One may be as poor as church mice, but, hiring help to serve at Table is a must. Four courses are usually served: an *entrée*, a fish dish, *le plat*, followed by the dessert. Salad is served, but salad dressings are unknown – if you like limp tatty lettuce you're in luck! There is no rush to replace one course with the next because, in our case certainly, diminutive French kitchens invite congestion with more than four empty plates, and the dishwasher full with six. This was a case where logistical necessity drove social norms. These intervals, with mouths empty but the wine flowing, are used for discussing absent diplomatic personalities or putting the World straight. If you have a French lady next to you, be sure that you ask the first question – this ensures that you will at least know what the subject of conversation is for the first minute and a half. The rest of her discourse will involve a torrent of impeccable subjunctives at a rate which seems to dispense with any need for breathing – but which nonetheless leaves you speechless. You will also have very little idea of what was said! Just sit back and enjoy the food, refresh you glass, and flirt with your wife at the other end of the table – do not feel obliged to entertain your lady companions for they will be quite content to do so all by themselves. As the evening winds down, Americans are the first to show signs of wear looking furtively at their watches, offering lame excuses about the desperate plight of their baby sitters or an early rise upon the morrow for a 7am staff meeting---non Americans haven't the foggiest notion of what they are talking about since 7.00am is an hour which does not register in their consciousness. Like Cinderella on the stroke of twelve, the evening is tacitly brought to a close at midnight, and feeling very contented the guests go out into the night, while the hosts are happy just to collapse!

During this early period I had to leave Helga in Paris alone on occasion but she is a resourceful person and coped extremely well. On one such occasion we were to have a meeting of the CRD in Los Alamos, and Don Kerr had arranged to show off some of his favorite "toys"."Toys", in this context, refer to huge and complex machines which occupy a whole building. Ulf Lantzke, and his assistant Bill Martin, both wanted to take advantage of this opportunity. Ulf ,very sportingly, wanted to go by Concorde and I was not about to dissuade him. We caught the eleven o'clock plane, and after a very fine lunch landed in New York in time for breakfast at eight-thirty. It was the only time in my life I ever saw the sun go down in the East! Complaints about the Concorde only appear to come from those who have never been on it. I am a fan! From Kennedy airport, we transferred to La Guardia and took a plane to Dallas. On the way there occurred a moment I shall never live down. When we were going over the Blue Ridge Mountains of Virginia I looked down and saw Wintergreen. I was quite excited, and said to Bill Martin "Look Bill, I have a place right down there". "Which side of the plane?, asked Bill. "The right side", said I, and he dutifully looked down. In about an hour we were entering Texas, and Bill said to me,"Look Eric, there's my place down there". "Which side of the plane?", said I. "Both sides",said Bill – and he meant it! It transpired that he owned more oil property in Texas and Oklahoma than you could possibly imagine.

There was an interesting little post script to this trip. Helga had written down a request for me to bring back some item she wanted. I could not then, nor can I now, read Helga's writing. Nor for that matter can anyone else. I think it is for that reason that nobody has received a letter from Helga in the past I don't know how many years.

Eric H. Willis

When passing through Denver, I asked a colleague if we could visit a Supermarket to make my purchase. We studied Helga's hieroglyphics and agreed that the item in question was most likely to be "Fit and Trim", dog food for Putzi. It seemed to make sense – obviously it was unobtainable in Paris, but all the dogs on Paris streets leave ample evidence that they are well fed, *n'est-ce pas*? Not to worry, we duly bought twenty pounds of the stuff, and pushed it into a reluctant suitcase. I lugged this load through Houston before returning to Paris, where I proudly presented my trophy to Helga. "But I wanted Dexitrim for me" said Helga, "Not Fit and Trim for Putzi". This was a diet supplement whose packet weighed four ounces at the most. Oh Dear -- but dear old Putzi had food for a while!!

17. Winter Sports.

I do not know quite what possessed us -- we had to have been inflicted with the March Hare Syndrome, or some such malady. We decided we would take a week off, and go skiing. We chose a nearby European venue, just a thousand kilometers away in *Seefeld*, Austria! To compound the felony, we also decided to drive. I bought some ski racks which relied on webbing straps to hold them on the roof. I made the mistake of putting them on wet. Everything was fine until the straps dried out and stretched, and we were on the German Autobahn when the load started to shiver and shake. This would be a great place for the whole lot to fall off

We decided that we would take off on Friday afternoon and stop over for the night in Strasbourg. The Autoroute to Strasbourg is fast, and at that time there was comparatively little traffic. In fact it is a beautiful road which invited a certain amount of, shall we say, competitive speed. Suffice to say that we covered the five hundred kilometers in five hours even, including a generous pit stop and a cup of coffee. Putzi woke up and got excited as we drew into the City; she had an uncanny knack of knowing we had arrived at our destination. However, she had one failing – she did not want to pee in strange places, and we had to march her up and down a Park in order to get her to oblige.

The next day we left via the Autobahn to Stuttgart where we found that the much vaunted highway could also be reduced to a standstill while a winding hill was negotiated by slow moving trucks. This cost us an hour and a half. I am happy to say that this bottle neck has since been removed. Eventually, we turned off at Ulm for Kempton and Füssen, and where we had a fine lunch at a hostelry beside a lake in the countryside. It was one of those places, with "Germany" written all over it, which are immensely attractive with their heavy oak doors, wooden beams, and tiled floors. Eventually we crossed the Austrian border and descended into the Inn Valley, arriving in Seefeld just before dusk with the odometer reading 999 kilometers.

The Inn was quite delightful and friendly. There were one or two things to get used to. On the breakfast table was a decorated basket, which we learned was there to put all the debris from the meal, such as one peels off butter, jam, sugar etc. You found the table spotless, and you leave it spotless: transgressors are politely but firmly reminded of this fact. This IS Austria, and compliance is a must. Seefeld is a pretty village, with lovely chalets, Bauernmalerei paintings on the walls, and onion dome churches. Putzi again took a dislike to peeing without familiar smells, and we had to find a patch of snow free grass near the Bahnhof to satisfy her. The scenery is majestic, and I suppose that if you were a good skier you would have a ball on the slopes. I was beginning to reconcile myself to the fact that I would never make the Olympic Team – of any nation. The Seefeld experience only confirmed this hunch. Helga, I have to painfully admit, is far more accomplished than I, although that in itself does not put her in the first rank just behind Jean Claude Killey. We decided to take group lessons, Helga taking an intermediate class, while I acknowledged my limitations by joining a beginners group. I was the last person in the line of students, all youngsters with no inhibitions about broken bones and the consequences thereof. Of course, with the gyrations which were asked of us, I fell – maybe a few times. My instructor, a fellow I now stereotype as "uncompromising Austrian", was less than sympathetic. His sole contribution to my progress was the friendly admonition, "What are you doing down there, you Fool? Get up!" When you are in your fifties, and trying desperately to learn something with demonstrably little aptitude, such comments are singularly unhelpful. They are even downright discouraging. My attitude to this fellow, I have to confess, was extrapolated to the somewhat pompous Austrian Ambassador to the OECD – dear old Count Pumpernickel. We ventured for an excursion along the Inn valley as far as Innsbruck, and were most impressed; I was resolved to go back sometime, but in summer when skiing instructors are busy scything their *Almen*. I will go up to him and say" What are you doing down there, you Fool? Haven't you heard of a Weed Whacker!" Then he would stretch his aching back and he'd be sorry, so he should!

We started our trip back to Paris via *Neu Schwanstein,* mad *König Ludwig's* fairy tale castle which has been hijacked by Disney as its theme park motif. Actually, the castle is not old at all, but no matter, it is a splendid sight. It was climbing up to this castle via a steep driveway where we ran into "Flo", our fictional character we had invented in Grindelwald back in August. This version of "Flo" was quintessentially unlovely and her equally unlovely son was making a nuisance of himself on a snow covered grass slope towards the wall. "Flo" was displeased -- she harnessed all of the generous lung capacity that God had given her for one spectacular explosion. "Dai- veee. Were are you, Dai-veee!" resonated around the mountain at force ten, which shattered not only the pristine silence but all glass within a ten mile radius. What a classic!

We elected to take a different route back to Strasbourg, and cut down south from Stuttgart towards the Black Forest. We stayed the night at a small picturesque town called Herrenberg at a very clean B & B for the very modest sum of forty seven deutschmarks. In the evening we went out to a small gasthof to have a very pleasant but simple dinner. We sat at the scrubbed communal table with a young man who engaged in conversation with Helga. He was flattered that someone of Helga's, shall we say, age, would even talk to him and very politely pointed out that since he was only seventeen he should be addressed more appropriately as "*Du*" instead of "*Sie*". I cannot think of an equivalent in English, but in an old fashioned way it was most touching. The next day took us through the heart of the *Schwarzwald* to *Freudenstadt,* where we were later to spend many happy days and walk many happy miles. It became a Mecca for us, and we came to know the area, with its *Wanderweg* system, very intimately. From there it was a straight shot through Strasbourg once more, where we had lunch, and on to Paris – and home!

Future skiing excursions were to be in the French Alps. There we met an instructor who was patient, kind, and quite able to cope with our limited skiing abilities! An inspiring friend -- not a drill Sargent! What a pleasure skiing can be!!

18. Berlin in Springtime – A Strangled City.

It was early April, and the sun was shuffling off its long slumber. The Conservation Working Group of the IEA, under John Millhone's, (DOE), chairmanship, had worked most diligently for about a year to present a large conference on Conservation Technologies. John had secured and donated the services of a contractor to mange the arrangements, and they were certainly needed for the conference site was to be in Berlin and the logistics would have been beyond the capacity of any part time group. On my staff, the credit unquestionably goes to Bernd Kramer, who was imaginative and diligent throughout, especially when it came to compiling the Proceedings which he did almost single handedly.

I had never been to Berlin, and so the prospect was at the same time exciting at going there but apprehensive about the outcome. The IEA had staked a lot of reputation on this conference, and gained considerable backing from both the City and the Federal German Government. Berlin was still a divided city torn apart by that excrescence, the Berlin Wall. Anyone who has ever seen, let alone lived with, this monument to Communism will remember it forever. It was designed to both keep ideas from the people, and to keep its citizens locked within the tentacles of its ruthless regime. The number who died horribly trying to escape is all too many; the gap between the wall and the East Berlin secondary wall was an open area about a hundred yards wide which was criss-crossed with "dragons teeth" obstacles and easily raked by machine guns in the control towers. The famous Brandenburg Gate was barricade off at the dividing line – access to and from the Western Zone of Free Berlin and the East Zone was controlled by check points, the most famous of which was "Check Point Charlie" where spies were ceremoniously exchanged.

The demographics of the City reflected the realities of living there. It was the province of either the young or the old: the middle generation had fled to more prosperous pastures in West Germany. Access to the City was confined to the controlled Autobahn or flight corridors into *Tegel* Airport. The result was a disturbing air of artificiality. There were plenty of squatters in the old apartment houses, and the old Berliners patronized the *Tee Tanz*, with an air of resigned nostalgia, in the rebuilt *Kapinski* Hotel. The main thoroughfare, the *Kurfürstendam*, still sported the burnt out skeleton of the old church, *die Frauen Kirche*, but also had some nice cafés, restaurants and stores. Our hotel, pretentiously called the "Europa", was away from the "classical" part of the City, near the site of the Convention Center where the Conference was being held. It was a dismal, gray post-war concrete structure of unrelieved gloom near the bus station. Helga protested the overpowering disinfectant smell in the room, but received little sympathy from the management. But it was convenient, and we stayed until the end of the week when we decamped for the *Kapinski*.

By contrast, the Convention Center was quite excellent. Besides featuring multiple sessions with ease, it had a very fine restaurant and facilities. The long concourse allowed administration to be handled efficiently, and participants the space to mix freely. I gave the Opening Address, and I am happy to note that my speech reflected the appropriate degree of hope that Technology would indeed help the all important reduction in demand which was to be so telling by 1985. I noted the prevailing view that conservation was not seen as all that sexy, with the words:

> "Rarely, and regretfully, is it viewed as a <u>positive</u> activity associated with the effective use of precious resource – there are always constant reminders of ways to use our <u>money</u> wisely, but to be reminded of how to use <u>energy</u>

wisely is regarded as somehow the constant reminder of
an unpleasant truth, and mildly distasteful".

The Sessions were immensely upbeat, and served to reverse the
popular perception of Conservation and restore it to its rightful place
in the armory against the OPEC stranglehold. The Proceedings were
published by Springer Verlag in three volumes, each an inch and
three quarters thick, and were widely distributed. As a fringe benefit,
the publishers gave John Millhone and me an honorarium of fifteen
thousand Deutschmarks. We both felt we had absolutely no claim to this
money ourselves, so after consulting the OECD lawyers it was agreed
to put it in a fund which would constitute representation funds for the
CRD when its members came to Paris for its meetings. We managed to
make this fund stretch just to the end of my tenure in1985.

Meanwhile Helga took the opportunity to take a tour to Potsdam,
in East Germany, while I had to wait for the weekend to savor a short
city tour which gave me a flavor of the Wansee area, which was the
infamous site of the "Final Solution" of the Jewish question. I left Helga
in Berlin to look around some more, and early on the Sunday morning
I took off from Tegel to make a connection in Frankfurt for Chicago.
As the plane lifted off over Berlin on that crystal clear morning, one
could see the entire wall in all its obscene clarity completely around
West Berlin. It looked like a gigantic band desecrating the landscape,
and was to stay there for another eight years. When was to later see
the stultifying effects of a centrally planned economy plus the brutal
repression that was perpetrated upon these people, one wonders how
Communism ever survived for so long. The answer lay in the mind
set and ruthlessness of such bullies that perpetrated monstrosities like
the wall I was seeing right below me right now. When Reagan spoke
of the "Evil Empire", he was not far off the mark. Lest the passage of
time allows readers of today to think even remotely benign thoughts
about the Communist Era, the brutality of the period was a blight on
civilization. We were fortunate that the Iron Curtain fell without a shot
being fired. What a blessing!

19. The Weevil in the Bedroom – Snoring

It must have started the previous July when I caught the Paris Crud. Or maybe it was back in 1953 when I smashed my nose well and truly playing that gentle game of cricket. Whatever caused it happened; I started to snore. Now the snorer is usually blissfully convinced that he is sleeping like a baby, but for anyone else living under the same roof, a pride of lions devouring a herd of gazelles could not make more grunting noises with such deadly effect. Helga discovered this small shortcoming of mine in M_rren the previous August, and while in Berlin it appeared obvious that something had to be done about it. There is not much melody in snoring, and no such thing as "Love me, Love my snore".

One of the problems of going to the doctor in France is explaining exactly what is wrong with you. You have to spend some time with the dictionary rehearsing your body parts. *Ronfler* is to snore, *tousser* is to cough, and *la narine* is a nostril. The problem, as always, is that asking the questions is not the problem; it is understanding the answer. By chance, my old school friend from England, Don Anniss and his wife Cath visited us in Paris, and I was describing my dilemma. Don was a family doctor in Brighton on the South Coast of England, and I thought perhaps that he might know someone through his practice who would have some ideas. "I know the perfect fellow", said Don,

"His nurse is a great friend of ours". By traveling to England I could see a top notch specialist who actually spoke my native language. Ideal.

I duly flew to Gatwick Airport, hired a car, and traveled the thirty-five miles down to Brighton to stay with the Anniss's overnight. The next afternoon, at two o'clock, Don escorted me to the great man's house. He was a somewhat distant fellow, but his nurse was a most pleasant lady. Don had told her of my coming, so both of them knew who I was and what the problem was. He sat me down in a chair and squirted something up my nose, which went suitably numb. Noses are sensitive things, and don't take kindly to intrusions with pieces of metal unless properly prepared. He pronounced that there was no apparent damage from the cricket injury, no blockage of the nasal passages, nor was the septum deviated in the slightest. Furthermore, since he could find nothing wrong, there was nothing he could prescribe. With this splendid diagnosis of impeccable nasal health, I was still left with my nocturnal malady.

Never mind, it was a splendid April afternoon, and I got in the car for the pleasant drive to my Mother's house, two miles short of Gatwick Airport. My concerns about the snoring seemed to evaporate. As I joined the main A23 road heading north, I was acutely aware of just what a splendid afternoon this was. The sun was shining, the sky was blue, the birds were chirping, the grass was green, and I did what I was normally forbidden to do, I sang my heart out. It was a great day to be alive, and I was determined to make the most of it. The windows were down, the wind was blowing through my hair, the cars going by me had the full benefit of my melodies and I was convinced I was making their day for them. What a happy little fellow they must think me!

About three miles from my Mother's, I began to sneeze, a little at first, and then constantly. By the time I reached Mother's, I could not stop. I felt really bad by now, and saying a rapid goodbye to my Mother, I headed for the airport because I had to be in Bonn, Germany, the next day. I checked in the car, and got the plane for the hour flight to Paris. I managed to drive from Charles de Gaulle by sheer will power, and staggered into the apartment. Helga was aghast. "My God", she said,"You only went to get your nose looked at, and you end up a basket case!" Needless to say, I did not go to Bonn the next day, as Helga nursed me back to sanity. What had happened remained a mystery. I just could not explain it, but put it down to some strange allergy, and forgot about it.

About five weeks later it was the Whitsun Holiday. Helga thought it might be fun to spend a few days in Normandy. We found a place commensurate with our budget modestly called *La Bellevue*, in a small village on the coast called *Villerville*, ten kilometers along from *Honfleur*. It was somewhat faded, and certainly dated – *Monsieur Hulot* would have been quite at home there. It was here that we had our first dish of *"Friuts de Mer"*. One is presented with a huge dish of shells, crustaceans, and other anonymous creepy crawlies. I will say that they make sure you are fully equipped for the task of extracting whatever lies inside these creatures. The "kit" includes pins, long and short, and various bent rods all too reminiscent of what had been shoved up my nose recently. At the end of a triumphant hour you have a dish full of empty shells to show for your pains, but you still feel in need of a good meal!

We traveled along the coast through *Deauville and Trouville* ,where Helga was later to spend more time at a spa. We passed all those famous Normandy beaches linked to the Invasion of 1944, but everything was shut so we headed on to Bayeux where we had lunch. At lunch, we made a small discovery. Normandy is so named because it was populated by Norsemen in the Tenth Century, and every person in the restaurant had blue eyes, and this observation was confirmed while walking around the town. The Bayeux Tapestries, depicting the Battle of Hastings in 1066, were what we had come to see, and they were even more descriptive and detailed than I had ever imagined. They go around three sides of the room depicting scenes of the preparation for the Invasion, the Crossing of the Channel, the Battle, and the triumph of King William. Furthermore, it is in splendid condition. We have a reproduction of one panel of the tapestry in our home in Arlington, depicting the crossing of the Channel. I am in favor of such reproductions if they remind you lovingly of your visit to see the real thing!

This visit to Normandy provided an unexpected revelation concerning my strange behavior after visiting the Ear, Nose and Throat specialist in Brighton six weeks previously. Don and Cath Anniss were also visiting *Honfleur* over Whitsun and we arranged to meet them there for Sunday lunch at the *Cheval Blanc* on the *Quai des Passagers* facing the old harbor. Their friend, the nurse with the Ear, Nose, and Throat specialist was there too with her husband. Over lunch, I happened to mention my experience on leaving his house a month earlier. "Didn't he tell you, she said," he put straight cocaine powder up your nose!". Now they tell me!!. I do not know what I would do on a lie detector test....... "well I, umph, tried it once, I inhaled it, I even liked it...." Sure, a likely story, but only Presidents get away with that one – and besides, I was still snoring!

What to do now? There was nothing left but to take one's chances with the French. Back to the dictionaries, and endless rehearsals. I consulted our doctor, Doctor Fodor, who by now we had seen often enough with the Paris Crud to trust. Besides, her English was impeccable. She said that her son had had a similar problem, and that an ENT man in the Sixth Arrondissment had proved quite effective. If she appeared somewhat skeptical of ENT men, I, with my recent experience, was positively jaundiced. The Doctor in question lived on *Rue Simon*, off *Boulevard St. Germain*. His *cabinet* ran true to form – it was in a dingy apartment up the predictable staircase with the now standard threadbare carpet. We came to two conclusions

> i] that there must be a speciality supply store somewhere in Paris that specializes in the outfitting of fully faded Doctor's Offices, and

> ii], that the essential qualifications for faithful retainers who answer doors to Doctor's Offices must be that they are both vocally monosyllabic and visually expressionless.

Eric H. Willis

The room into which we were ushered made Dr Fordor's waiting room look the epitome of the modern age. If transported lock, stock, and barrel to the United States, I am sure it would have raised a small fortune. But here in its proper setting, it looked what it was – a collection of old pieces that now looked like, shall we say,, junk. In a while, ponderous footsteps on the wooden floor heralded the imminent arrival of Doctor Autier. Dr. Autier was of some indeterminate age above seventy -five. He was about six foot five, and would have done well scaring young children in a fairground haunted house. He had a bare boned skull, steel framed glasses, and a cadaverous demeanor. He opened the door to the accompaniment of onomatopoeic creaking. His cavernous voice uttered "Monsieur Willis !!!" in a cadence which offered nothing but doom – he could well have had a noose in his hand. I followed him into what was his Office. In fact, the *Conciergerie* in *Marie Antoinette's* day had nothing to match it. The patient's chair was made of metal, and covered in what had originally been white enamel. He proudly informed us that he had inherited it from his father. The arm rests terminated in two vertical handles, polished down to the bare metal by the terrified grip of generations of patients convinced of impending and inevitable pain. His equipment would have done a soothsayer in the darkest Amazon proud. They were contained in an old metal cigar box, the pattern on which had been worn down to a few unrecognizable fragments; its contents were an assortment of metal prods bent to achieve penetration of the nasal cavities. He had a stool in front of the patient on which he sat with a mirror and a light on a band around his head. With his lanky frame bent almost in two, he then peered into your nostrils. There was no need for anesthetic because your state of induced psycho-paralysis beat out any dose of cocaine. He saw that the nasal passages were constricted, and that the septum had been deviated at some point. So much for the British Wizard! -- we were now back to my own self diagnosis. He thought, and I think he was right, that there were allergies at work here. He quizzed me on this, and I replied that yes, I sneezed when I had whisky or chocolate. He dutifully inscribed on a 3x5 card – *whisky et chocolat.* He prescribed some desensitizing, which entailed my being jabbed in the butt at weekly intervals by the Nurse at the OECD.

The condition improved for a while, to the point when I told him *"Vous avez sauvez ma marriage!"* – the fact that I was not yet married was beside the point. By this time we got to know this character a bit better, and it turned out that he was still an active mountaineer and skier, and he was someone to be admired. In fact we came to rather like him, and once his face actually allowed itself a smile.

Alas, it did not last, and he decided that the roto-router was the only effective remedy for lasting relief. By this time, I was ready for anything -- bring on the rack! It involved enlarging the nasal passages by cauterization. This is medicalese for burning the damn things out with a red hot poker! On the appointed day, I assumed my place in the dreaded chair, and he produced some electrical equipment last used by Thomas Edison. There was an old fashioned frayed wire attached to ceramic terminals which I had not seen in fifty years; it ended in a crude filament which he inserted into my nose like a soldering gun.. When the current was turned on, there was an awful choking smell of my own flesh burning. However drastic the remedy, it worked. After the carnage up my nose healed, the positive effect was immediate. It was thus with some confidence that I went back a month later to have the other nostril done in the same distasteful way. It did the trick – the Bedroom Weevil was vanquished.

Twenty years later they do it with lasers, and you don't feel a thing! Now it is Helga who drives one from the room!

20. Political Winds of Change – and their effects on IEA research

It was difficult to believe that a whole year had gone by since I had first arrived in Paris. Here were the horse chestnuts out in full bloom once again, just as they had been on the first evening when I had sauntered through *Les Jardins de Ranelagh* – how different the political complexion had become just twelve months later. The American Election of 1980 had brought in a highly conservative Republican government under Reagan dedicated to free market principles and an abhorrence of anything which they thought savored of industrial policy. The ground rules were changed completely. There was even talk of the Department of Energy itself being abolished, being seen as the foremost advocate of interventionist policies. In Bonn, the Helmut Schmidt government was still center left and leaned towards the very policies being now eschewed by Washington. It too was destined for a short life as the Christian Democrats came to power later in the year. Budget constraints later exacerbated the problem. The IEA, and the research activities it had embraced in the late seventies, clearly had to adapt to these changing circumstances. Nevertheless, I did not particularly relish defending Washington against the capricious ideological dictates of low level functionaries. This led to three meetings in Germany in rapid succession which reflected, in their own way, the strains brought about by the conflicting policies of two major players, Washington and Bonn.

(i)   Politics in Bonn

It was important to get to know the principal figures in the Energy Ministry (BMFT) in Bonn on a more personal basis. Germany was a staunch supporter of the IEA, and the Director of Research of the BMFT had been the Chairman of our own CRD prior to my friend Don Kerr. His name was Wolf Schmit-K_ster – I had spoken to him on the phone, but had not met him, and it was important that I do so, particularly to get the German reaction to the changing energy policy direction in Washington. Accordingly, I asked my colleague Bernd Kramer to make arrangements for a meeting in Bonn with his old boss.

Bonn lies on the Rhine where it flows through more gentle country after leaving the dramatic Gorge area. I like Bonn, but am not so enamored with its climate. Maybe I just have plain bad luck, but the river valley seemed to have a micro climate of its own; rainy, misty, and humid. I had first passed through the City in 1953, when people were still living under tarpaulins strung from the remaining walls of bombed out buildings – what a transformation to see it rejuvenated. As a town, it is just about the right size, and has a lot of charm in the older parts. One particular place to visit, as if to do homage, is the Beethoven Haus where Beethoven grew up. It was adopted as the seat of Government of West Germany, the Federal Republic, and was ringed with Ministries while mostly retaining its own character. Germany, for understandable utilitarian reasons shared by many countries recuperating from the war, had a phase of putting up low cost structures with little or no redeeming features. That era had in turn been replaced by a period of imaginative construction which, with some very good landscaping, had served to make a most attractive city. Now that the reunified Germany has changed its Capital to Berlin, Bonn has been reduced in importance to some extent. But it has enough character of its own to survive.

We arrived in the late afternoon, and stayed at a hotel we were to stay in on many subsequent occasions, the *"Kurf_rstenhof"* in *Popplesdorf Allee*. Our host for the evening was an old friend who had been the German Science Attaché in Washington, Werner Minden.

We had a splendid dinner, and a good evening of wine sipping in a *weinstube*. It was quite a shock to find out what the cost of German wines was in Germany!

My meeting in the the BMFT had an undercurrent of tension. For the first time since Schmidt-Kuster had been associated with the IEA six years ago, he was palpably uneasy with the way things were going. The source of the tension was partly political and partly economic.

The complexion of the German Government at that time was center / left -- the Social Democrats were in power. They tended to lean more to government intervention which implied active leadership, on the grounds that they, not industry, were responsible for the economy as a whole. The new American Government had shifted markedly right, and their more conservative bent eschewed making industrial policy and was inclined to leave what they felt to be market place decisions to industry. This divergence of views directly impacted attitudes towards the pursuit of synthetic fuel research, which was getting increasingly expensive with projects far outstripping their original cost projections. It is not just technical success which was at issue, investors have a keen eye to the financial results too. In summary was research to be government driven, or market driven? In May1981, it was not clear which way the argument would go, but as the year progressed it was clear that until there was more awareness of what was involved in these complex technical projects, and the price tags associated with them based on realism, it was doubtful what investor group or corporate board was going to sanction a project with widely uncertain costs and of uncertain duration.

The other source of tension was an economic one, which was affecting Germany's ability to engage in international projects on a large scale which involved dollars. From a low point the previous year, the dollar had appreciated rapidly against the European currencies, and would continue to do so until it reached almost crisis proportions in 1985, when a meeting of the G-7 countries tackled the problem. The price of oil had been rising steadily at the same time as the dollar had been appreciating. Since the price of oil was denominated in dollars, the price of oil in European national currencies almost doubled. This added further strain on their international current account balances caused by the original price hike in the first place. The result was cut backs by governments on projects in which they would be obligated to pay precious dollars to fund their share. Governments were preferring instead to enter into projects in which they contributed their share in kind and thus paid for it in their own domestic currencies. These cost shared projects are not the easiest projects to manage, accountability is difficult, and hit at the heart of the IEA collaborative research program.

The conversations that morning were personally friendly, but while we could help define the problem we were not in a position to solve it. They were a good preparation for me, however, for the Symposium in Frankfurt the following Monday. Mulling over the morning, I joined Helga for lunch with our US Science Counselor to Bonn, Bob Morris, at the US Embassy on the shores of the Rhine. I had first met Bob in Moscow, and then again in Paris when I first arrived. He was an experienced hand, but he thought the political landscape was changing rapidly. I was anxious to maintain the best possible relations with our German colleagues, and had no wish to make it more complicated for them. The Government of Helmut Schmidt fell within a short time, and was replaced by the more conservative government of Helmut Kohl. They were somewhat less interventionist than the Schmidt government had been, and were less inclined to fund mammoth synthetic fuels projects. Nevertheless, the underlying financial tensions due to the oil price were to remain until the oil price started to fall, and the dollar too, in 1985.

(ii)   Synfuels in Frankfurt

Synthetic fuels were now one of the items of major disagreement between Washington and Bonn. Bonn still supported them, while Washington wanted to abandon all funding for them – immediately, no matter any prior commitments that had been made to our allies in the IEA. The charge of unreliable ally was not far from the surface among American friends.

Eric H. Willis

True to form, there was now a weekly newsletter devoted to synthetic fuels which catered to this hot topic. Newsletters seemed to spring up like mushrooms in the night, particularly when governments were pouring large sums of money into energy projects. The newsletter was to have a symposium on the subject of synthetic fuels in Frankfurt on May 11th, and would I give a speech? The High Level Group on Commercialization of Alternative Fuels, commissioned under the Carter presidency, was to submit its Final Report the following week, and so the subject of the Symposium was topical. It was also somewhat controversial, since the new Administration in Washington had shown itself to be markedly antipathetic to major public sector investments in Synthetic Fuels. The newsletter would undoubtedly report on its own meeting, and the content of its next issue might as well be taken from one's own input as from sheer speculation. In the event this happened, and the publication duly summarized the proceedings invoking the phrase"....Willis said...." fourteen times on one page!

I have a copy of the speech I gave at the meeting, and one paragraph caught my eye as I reread it:

" It has often been said that you can take a horse to water but you can't make it drink. It may well be that governments can create favorable climates for their industrial horses to drink, but is that industry thirsty enough to oblige the government gestures? The role of governments in this dilemma is really at the crux of the matter. Can they create the climate convincingly enough today, and can the industrial horses see enough thirst in tomorrow, to induce even modest sipping now? If they cannot, which seems increasingly likely, then the springboard for the nineties will be a shaky one indeed".

The answer to my question turned out to be no – the springboard was non existent. Governments were not in a position to induce industry to play along, and the oil price lowering in 1985 sealed their fate. Industry is always willing to sip at the public trough when money is to be made from government funding, but their own money – No!

I left the meeting somewhat disillusioned, to say the least. The meeting was held at the Frankfurt Intercontinental Hotel, a graceless building designed to reassure Americans that they had never left New York. There was not an atom of "Germanness" about it, and another and less expensive venue might have been chosen. The persons on site managing the meeting seemed overtly more worried about making a profit than providing a genuine forum for the discussion of synfuels. This attitude was almost a guarantee of superficiality. The audience had paid hefty fees for the privilege of hearing the likes of me, and the cost to the conveners for the services of at least this speaker was nearly zero---my "fee" was a ball point pen! As far as I could tell, the audience did not come from the synfuel industry itself, but from the merely curious with peripheral interests---the discussion was desultory. Nevertheless, it did provide good exposure for the IEA's activities in the field, and this is often of value in itself. On this occasion anyway, my speech was appropriate, and viewed from a perspective of so many years later, most prescient,

(iii) Coal in Düsseldorf.

In contradistinction to the Synfuels Meeting in Frankfurt, the IEA sponsored Coal Conference held in Düsseldorf was a scientific gathering of practitioners in the field. The host organization, to whom many thanks were in order, was *Bergbau-Forschung*, the principal German Coal Research Institute.

Coal had been badly neglected, and in the scientific doldrums; such a conference had not been held in thirteen years. It came as a surprise to the organizing committee that over one hundred and fifty papers were submitted for presentation during a three day period by attendees from around the world. The papers described only basic coal science, and not the technologies of coal conversion or its utilization. Thus the new American Administration did not oppose its being held

Coal is so easily taken for granted, but which is in fact a complex chemical marvel. There is absolutely no substitute for a well prepared gathering of active practitioners rather than the contrived machinations of a "for profit" venture, such as the debacle in Frankfurt, thrown together as a target of opportunity. Both the Berlin Conference on Conservation and this one amply proved the point. As an aside, I did have the honor of bringing to the podium two German ladies, from among the diners at the formal dinner, to take a well earned bow holding hands . They had been pioneers and pre-eminent in basic coal science back in the thirties. They were, of course, retired by that time, and they appeared gracious beyond belief. To my dismay, I found out later that despite the magnanimous show that each had put on they had disliked each other intensely for nearly five decades!! Fools rush in!!

21. Living in a Parisian Microcosm ....Apartment Dwellers.

Outside the Living Room of our home in Arlington, there is an azalea hedge which in Springtime is a magnificent show of large pale purple flowers. In Winter, when it is bereft of leaves, the hedge is populated once again by a colony of sparrows. There are cheeky ones, shy ones, gregarious ones, raucous ones, imperious ones, funny ones, fussy ones, and taken together they constitute a microcosm of avian society. Every time I watch their antics, it has an uncanny resemblance to apartment living in Paris. Apartment living is rather like a large nesting box; each inhabitant being preoccupied with his own life and living out his own character, hopes and dreams.

This was the first time in my life that I had lived in an apartment – interactions with people who lived around you were a mystery to me. I was like the sparrow who had never had to live in the "hedge". Helga, on the other hand, had spent some time in the "hedge" at one period in her life. Helga is more gregarious than I, naturally inquisitive, and genuinely concerned about people. This proves a remarkable asset in adjusting to apartment living. There is one golden rule in Paris apartments – Silence! This is not just refraining from making noises that irritate other people, but the stoic silence when one meets the same person in the elevator for years. One has not been introduced: since there is no one around to perform this function, stony silence reigns. The log jam is broken only when a chirpy "sparrow" like Helga arrives on the scene, and the building was a different place after her arrival.

Helga found the magic formula for making friends through walking our dog. There is no question but that Putzi was a magnificent specimen, and always attracted attention. She seemed to know it too, and she was soon termed *"La Fifi Parisienn"*. Every evening about ten o'clock, a group of dog owners would congregate outside the front door of the building. This little seance was a ritual attempt to get the dogs to relieve themselves before nightfall, but it became a pleasant social gathering on the sidewalk. Much to the consternation of the assembled group, Putzi would march in a circle around them, perform, and considering her mission accomplished continue on and re-enter the front door. Consternation was followed by admiration, and admiration by friendliness – join the Club Madame! In no time at all, Helga was with the "in" group. Putzi was a great ambassador, and seemed to enjoy charming the local shopkeepers bringing Helga in her tow to introduce her!

As mentioned earlier, the key to knowing what is going on in any apartment complex is the *Concièrge*. We had a gem: Madame Sanier. Her first name was Louise, but one would never dream of addressing her as such. Mme Sanier was a smart woman, and managed to buy a few studio apartments in one wing of the building as an addition to her income and for her retirement. One such apartment was rented to a young woman she took under her wing, just as a protective "aunt" might. I could never make out why it was that this most attractive person dressed in a beautiful mink stole and very high heels should always be going to work at the same time each day – 6.30pm. Helga put me straight. The woman suddenly disappeared one day, and Mme Sanier explained to Helga that her unforgiving Corsican Mafia husband was about to be released from prison and would be on the prowl, so she had taken off in a hurry bordering on panic. A pity: she provided great local color., was a sweet person, and loved Putzi.

All *concièrges* get on with their building's inhabitants either by exercising total disdain, often portrayed in movies , or by taking people as you find them. Madame Sanier was one of the latter. She accommodated the most divergent of personalities, habits, and customs. As she explained to us once:

> *"Dans notre bâtiment, il y a:*
> *Monsieur le Monsieur, et*
> *Monsieur la Madame.*
> *Madame le Monsieur, et*
> *Madame la Madame"*

Although her description spanned the full range of sexual preferences, she was also implying that her "*bâtiment*" was a live and let-live society, which is to a great extent a reflection of Parisian society as a whole

Helga instituted "Open House" occasions, such as July 4th, when we included some of the neighbors surrounding our own apartment. This was something of a novelty to them: one just did not expose one's home to strangers. The "locals" dutifully came, whether out of a genuine spirit of bonhomie or merely to see if their suspicions about how Americans lived would be confirmed. Our elevator bank had two apartments to each landing, and we found ourselves introducing the Monsieur on the 6th floor right to the Monsieur on the 6th floor left for the first time. Now they could greet each other in the elevator at last!

The apartments on the 8th floor contained remarkably different characters. One was inhabited by an attractive blond forty-ish Swedish lady of liberal persuasion by the name of Yolande, who was in the publishing business. She gave us quite a few books, and I have to confess that I have just emptied them from my bookshelves unread after the intervening years. Yolande was in dire need of company, particularly male it would seem, but Helga and I as a couple would do in a pinch. Her neighbors in the adjoining apartment were a gentle older retired couple, the du Boisieu's. She was related in some way to the de Gaulle family, which provided a certain cachet. They invited us to their home on occasion, and it was a pleasant but somewhat formal affair. They commented, with a certain amount of distaste, on the Swedish lady Yolande next door. Of particular concern to them was the conduct of her love life. Apparently she was extremely audible, given to punctuating long sighs of joyful anticipation with orgastic shrieks of delight. The du Boisieux, now in their seventies, found all this rather disturbing, particularly at meal times.

No community is complete without its *bête noir*, somebody who everyone loves to dislike, and our community was no exception Our *bête noir* was unfortunately the inhabitant of the apartment below us. She became a widow while we were there, and she hardly broke stride in the process. She inherited a Yorkshire terrier from her husband that she used to lock up in a closet all day while she was out; it would cry incessantly, and that in itself did not endear her to Helga. It was reputed, by no less authority than the Concierge, that Mme. Bellancour had been a courtesan: the dictionary is quite explicit about the meaning of this term, so I will not elaborate because it was all too obvious. At one time she obviously had had good looks, but they had long ago been replaced by a permanent overlay of sheer malevolence. She was, as the saying goes, an overbearing, underbred, bore. On finally leaving the apartment to return to the US, we lowered an equally malevolent Mayan statuette onto her balcony. It was so evil looking that every maid we ever had, Paris or Washington, stood it in a corner with its face turned to the wall! We thought both Mme Bellancour and the statuette would now feel at home with each other.

The other side of the 9th floor landing lived two men, Claude and André, who befriended us in a most meaningful way. Claude was an architect, and André was a cardiologist. An evening in their apartment started with a magnificent dinner, and continued into the wee hours discussing the derivation of words. We would have dictionaries and encyclopedias all over the floor, and the hours just flew by. They were by far the people I felt most relaxed with to speak French, because they helped without being patronizing. They included us in their family gatherings, and this "inclusivity" was very important to Helga and me.

A *chaume*, or thatched cottage, is a special feature of Normandy and this one was just out of a picture postcard, with roses around the door and tall vibrant colored hollyhocks adorning the walls. It belonged to our neighbor on the 10th floor, Christian Flury. He was a widower, and we made good friends with him and his lady friend, Geneen, and he invited us down to his little *chaume* for the weekend. His wine cellar was excellent, and the sampling that weekend was, shall we say, extensive. Yes, we had quite a bit to drink. It would have been all right if he had not been an officiant at the old church adjoining his property. When the bell began to toll on the Sunday morning, it was right inside my head — if there is such a thing as purgatory, this was it. But at what seemed an ungodly hour in the morning, I dutifully went to mass with him.

The old priest was incomprehensible in any language, and he lost his way shortly after starting his homily. It would have been better if he had said "Amen" right there and then, but the old crusader in him made him march right on over the faithful in the pews, who from their glazed expressions were obviously deep in thought about more prosaic matters. Fatigue must have played its own merciful part, for in the middle of a sentence he invoked the Blessed Trinity and to the relief of all pronounced the Benediction.

I have to confess that my motives for attending mass were not entirely righteous, nor even altruistic. I was on a bizarre mission. What I wanted his signature on an affidavit saying that my son Nigel had been duly baptized in the Church. Without this certificate, Nigel could not get the local priest in New Jersey to agree to his marrying Lori, his fiancee, in the Catholic Church For some reason, this priest in New Jersey is not one of my favorite people.

In the Vestry after Mass, the Father said he would be happy sign it — in the afternoon! This was to be penance indeed! So, still nursing a hangover, we went along to his very humble abode about two o'clock. He truly lived in a small cell, with little of this world's trappings. He was just a wonderful fellow who wanted some company for a few hours – except, to my knowledge, he did not have a hangover. I hope the Good Lord will forgive me for the uncharitable thought that even the most obvious of Saints can be a trifle wearing, and the New Jersey brand incomparably more so. My priest friend finally obliged with his signature, and all was now in order to allow the Priest in New Jersey to marry Nigel and Lori in the American Catholic Church without bending his conscience one bit. Somebody owes me one for pulling this Rabbit out of the Hat!

Jean Nedjar was a Tunisian of Jewish extraction. He was our neighbor on the10th floor, and was just about as helpful as one could wish. On one occasion he generously gave us the use of his vacation apartment at *Juan les Pins* near *Antibes* on the Riviera. All the women, young and old, wore only the bottoms of their bikinis The costly strips of sand allotted to each person more resembled plots in a cemetery than places of enjoyment on a beach. All were" cheek to jowl", and afforded close proximity to some interesting sights.

On another occasion I was having a tussle with my travel agent and Cunard Lines over travel on the QE2. The time had come around when we were eligible to take home leave. The OECD had what I considered a very generous provision whereby one was given a fixed sum to take you there and back. How you traveled, and by what route, was your affair; this gave one a great degree of flexibility. The Cunard Line had advertised, in the International Herald Tribune, that on December 16th, the QE 2 would be sailing from Southampton for New York and thence to Fort Lauderdale, Florida. In this way we would be able travel as far as Miami, and to spend Christmas in Sarasota with Helga's Mother, Hertha. They were offering two for the price of one fares with return by British Airways. When I attempted to make reservations, Cunard took the position that this offer only applied to passengers originating in the United Kingdom. Jean Nedjar perused the "ad" in the "Trib", and pointed out that no mention was made of any such restriction. In his opinion it was false advertising. If need be,

I should sue. Next day, I told the travel agent that *mon advocat* had advised me to sue. This was pushing it a bit, but it worked a charm. By the end of that very same day, they had given me a first class cabin; I was very happy. By three weeks before sailing they had upgraded this to First Class Luxus, with an enormous cabin on Boat deck and dining in the Princess Grill; I was even more happy! Thank you Jean Nedjar! Of course, he wasn't really a lawyer but he knew enough to get me through that one!

The voyage was of course in mid-winter – not the season when chairs on deck demand heavy tips to the steward, or sun tan lotion is selling for a premium. With a force ten storm, it was hardly surprising that not a soul was to be seen on deck. One morning, I did venture out and nearly got my head blown off. I found that some enterprising individual had actually made a snow man out there, there was enough snow on the deck. Entertainment was definitely the preferred indoor pastime which involved such strenuous things as reading, sleeping, and some convivial drinking punctuated by gourmet meals. In the course of being "sociable", we had met a pleasant Californian couple. Since we had this fancy cabin on boat deck, it seemed we might act like mucky-mucks and ask them for pre-lunch drinks. The steward, an obliging sort of fellow, immediately took charge and organized a bar in our "living room" side of the cabin with glasses, hors d'oeuvres, and a fresh bottle of scotch. All was grandly set up, and all we had to do was to sit tight and wait for our guests to arrive. We were by now in mid-Atlantic, with nothing to see but the sea – a wintry gray sea at that. Idly glancing out of the large window that folks on boat deck are blessed with, I saw something which caught my eye on the roiling sea. It was a wave, but not any old wave; it was longer and higher than all the others, and what was more it coming steadily towards us. I called out to Helga, "Come and see this!" It was a strange thing to say, since she must have wondered what on earth there was to see in this horrible weather, and in mid-Atlantic. But nevertheless she did. We stood almost entranced, and certainly in awe at this solitary, and increasingly menacing, phenomenon in an otherwise bleak seascape. Then it hit! The entire ship was rolled to one side by the force, and this coupled with the angle of the cabin deck was such that all the preparations for pre lunch drinks were scattered as so many shards of broken glass and crumbs of hors d'oeuvres on the floor in a pool of whisky. A hideous mess! The steward was not fazed in the least little bit, quickly restored order, and brought a fresh supply of drinks and glasses in no time at all. All in a day's work! I The steward seemed to feel that, in true British tradition, nothing should get in the way of a pre-lunch cocktail party!

Communities are by no means confined to the building – by no means. They included *les dames du trottoir* who gathered like a taxi rank on the sidewalk opposite. They were there rain or shine, and it was not uncommon to see neighbors cross the road carrying hot drinks to them in the cold of winter. They were there for several years, and must have had a very satisfied clientele. Helga found that she was sharing hairdressers with one of them, so she felt she really was, to some extent, getting immersed in the local community. Another local feature was a small but very reputable second hand clothing boutique. Helga found me a fine sheepskin jacket, which I would be wearing today if only I could still get into it. But Helga's most notable purchase by far was her wedding dress – it was truly superb.

And so we were to spend five happy years among this cross section, not only of Paris but also the local *Quatier*. It gave us insights into Paris life we would not otherwise have had. The alternative would have been to inhabit some friendly ghetto of anglophones which many Americans prefer.. Our living in an all French apartment was our choice, and aided both in learning the language better and in understanding Parisian life, culture, and behavior patterns

22. Les Environs de Paris........ Weekend Haunts.

The Dictionary defines one meaning of "haunt" as a "Place of frequent resort". I thought that was a terse but quaint way of saying that since one likes a place so much, one goes there again and again. During the course of the Spring and Summer of 1981, Helga and I came to know a few spots around Paris that were so attractive as to become "haunts" over the next four years. The area around Paris is known as the *Île de France*; it contains a veritable treasury of cultural sites These sites ranged from cathedrals, to fortresses, chateaux, ruins, towns, and riverside villages. They were to become an enormous addition to our appreciation of Paris. What follows is not a travelogue – just our impression of some spots you might like to explore within an hour of Paris. References to fine eating places are, of course, an integral aspect of each site – they go together!

Chartres was one of the first to be explored, and is the farthest away. It lies eighty kilometers south-west of Paris, and the Cathedral can be seen standing proudly on a small butte as one approaches the town. It contains forty per cent of the World's remaining Mediaeval stained glass, from the 12th and 13th Centuries. They are said to contain five thousand images of people in one hundred and seventy six windows! On a bright day, the sun streams through the windows painting dancing spots of color on the bare flagstones worn smooth by centuries of footsteps. On the outside, the majestic flying buttresses proudly hold the one hundred and twelve foot high aisle in place, and with it the fan vaulted roof.

Many people have a hard time understanding how it is that a tall cathedral roof does not come falling down like a pack of cards. If it were not for one particular architectural feature it would, and this was brilliantly explained to the lay audience by an eccentric but knowledgeable guide who was a devotee of the Cathedral---he seemed to live and breath the place. He had a very convincing way of demonstrating how it worked. He selected four persons from his audience, and had them standing in pairs facing each other over a gap of about three feet. He then asked them to put one arm up, and then clasp the hand of the person diagonally across from him. The result was an arch of crossed arms. He then would asked a smaller person to grasp the point where the four arms met, and try to hoist themselves up. They <u>always</u> collapsed the arch of arms. He then asked four more persons to stand behind each of the four already standing facing each other, and to place one hand on the shoulders of the person in front of them, as if leaning gently against the shoulder. When the smaller person once more grasped the point where the four arms met, he was able to haul himself up <u>without</u> the arch collapsing. This very simple game gave everyone an understanding of how the flying buttresses outside the nave of the cathedral actually helped keep the roof in place. It was one fantastic lesson.

The present cathedral is, by comparison, rather modern stuff, for the base structure is Franco-Roman. *Chartres* draws me like a magnet; I can never visit it without an acute sense of awe. It is not just the age, for there are many structures which could compete on that score – it is rather the sheer beauty of the place, its proportions and its grace. There is a stained glass workshop close to the Cathedral which has achieved fame of its own. It furnished the entire stained glass for the East Window of the famous Salisbury Cathedral in England. This window is dedicated to the theme of "Prisoners of Conscience". And is as dramatic in its message as it is beautiful in its composition. We have a small stained glass piece from this *"atalier"* called a bouquet of flowers; it stands in the window of our home as the morning sunshine streams through, a constant reminder of *Chartres*.

My friend Jules Horowitz was a principal figure in the *Commisaireat de Energie Atomique*, and I got to know him for about a year or so while we were working together on a nuclear fusion project. Before he retired, Jules was far sighted enough to buy and totally restore a sixteenth century house in *Maintenon*, close by *Chartres*. When he invited me there one Sunday afternoon, I was quite unprepared. It was not just the history of the place, but the sheer underplayed elegance of the restoration which backed on to a small grass area and a flowing stream. The stream flows through the nearby *Chateau de Maintenon*. The fabric of the chateau is Renaissance style from the early fifteen hundreds. It was the home of *Françoise Scarron*, who was a paramour of Louis XIV, and became known as " *Madame de Maintenon*". My nuclear physicist friend had catholic tastes and good neighbors!

Versailles is renowned not only for its history, architectural beauty and the grandeur of its gardens. The ill fated Peace Treaty which regretfully bears its name is perhaps the only downside. Who can not be impressed, standing in front of the forecourt looking towards this incredible palace ! Nor who can walk through the Hall of Mirrors to admire that fine room in which so much history has been made, and which goes the whole length of the building facing the gardens? I will not add more to the many descriptions of its splendor, for they can be found in any guide book. What one can rarely see at Versailles, however, are the fountains in full display. The system which feeds them dates from the Louis XIV period, and requires the charging of a complex network of cisterns and syphons. The fountains are on display only a few days a year, and for a limited number of hours. While the Gardens are impressive enough, the addition of the Fountains in action leaves one gasping. It was in connection with the fountains that we have a special story.

Six of us, including Monika on a visit and our friends the Wettachs from Germany and their Son, decided to go to the performance of Handel's Water Music and the Royal Fireworks at the *Bassin de Neptune* in the Gardens. Since it had to be dark to stage the performance, a late dinner was called for as a fitting prelude. In front of the Courtyard of the Chateau, still in the town, there is a line of restaurants each with its outdoor tables along a gravel walk under a line of trimmed trees. It is almost unnecessary to say by now, but we had an excellent dinner, and towards the end I paid the bill by check, which is quite a normal thing to do in France. We left the restaurant, and strolled up to the *Bassin de Neptune* for the Performance. The lake and the fountains were colorfully illuminated and changed color as Handel's music ebbed and flowed. The performance culminated in the Firework Display which rose to a crescendo with the music. Marvelous!

Feeling that we had had a wonderful time, but not yet ready to call it a day, we made our way back to the same restaurant at which we had dined, in order to cap the evening with some dessert and some Cognac. As we approached the tables at which we had dined, three waiters were standing in the walkway with their hands belligerently on their hips, thunder in their faces, and retribution in their eyes. They allowed us to walk up to them without once changing either stance or expression. One of them at last proffered a chair, and we diffidently sat down. The ill will was palpable, and I finally said "Q'est-ce-q'espace?". One of them, his temper more in control than the others, explained to me somewhat forcefully that I had not paid the bill at Dinner, and they had been stuck with the cost! How dare we have the effrontery to come back! "That was not true", I said, "here is the stub of my Check". They murmured together in a huddle for a moment, and somewhat sheepishly went away leaving us feeling like pariahs. A short time later they returned, very humbly this time, one of them carrying my crumpled check, well marinated in the distilled essence of the evening's accumulated garbage! From a lynch mob to a reception committee was a pleasant transformation, and their offer of Cognac on the house was gladly accepted!

Do you believe in "Black Holes"? Helga does – in fact she has a pet one. North of Paris, not very far from Charles de Gaulle Airport, there is a lovely old town called *Senlis* with a fine but simple old Cathedral. It features prominently in French history and is replete with artefacts of long ago; the Kings of France made it their seat in the nine hundreds. The old town, with its cobbled streets and leaning houses, is something Disney has mercifully refrained from copying. The Cathedral was dedicated in 1191, so it has been around for a time. It does not boast of fine art inside, and the carving is plain but impressive. Neither is it besieged by endless bus loads, which is remarkable for being so near Paris. Its charm lies in the total picture; cathedral, houses, streets and history. Nevertheless, somebody has rendered it invisible! Despite her having been there three times to my knowledge, Helga maintains that she has never been there at all!. Please don't ask me to explain – I can't, but if you happen to be in that part of the world yourself, don't miss it!

Fontainblau is mostly associated with Napoleon, but that is not really being fair to *Fontainblau*. It has a long history going back to the fifteenth century. It does not look all that impressive from the courtyard, but the interior is outstanding. I will not dwell on the Chateau, great though it is. No, the great attraction for us was *Les Forêts de Fontainblau*, an enormous tract of land which was the scene of innumerable walks on a Sunday mornings among the famous *Rochiers*.. The *Rochiers* are weathered rock formations which provide challenging trails over a course that is designed to make you "puff". A sight that used to amuse us was the French folk who would enter the car park just off the main road, set up their chairs against the tail pipes of their cars, erect the picnic table, and eat lunch as if they had never left home. My, what they missed just behind them for they seldom ventured into the nearby forest. One saw few walkers on *les rochiers*, which suited us fine. However, the hike on a Sunday morning was merely a pleasant means of working up of an appetite for lunch at *L'Auberge de L'Île* at nearby *Le Samoir -sur-Seine*. This place was our Mecca – we loved it. Putzi loved it too, and obediently took her place under the table while we savored the delicacies. The owner, *M. Fernand*, had been the Chef on the French Liner "Normandie", and his dishes reflected his experience. On one occasion, a Great Dane decided to "smell Putzi out" under the table – so our very gentle dog snapped him! No fuss, he just backed off! The Seine flows leisurely past the front of this establishment, and the scene was one that Renoir could well have captured in his paintings.

By contrast, to the north of Paris there is an imposing, no a formidable, castle known as *Pierrefonds*. A Chateau of some sort has been standing on the knoll since the twelfth century, but alas the edifice before one is relatively modern. In 1813 Napoleon bought it for the paltry sum of 3000 francs – too bad he didn't have much time to enjoy it. It was restored completely in the realm of Napoleon III in 1857, so in relation to other antiquities around Paris the thing is just yesterday. Not to worry, despite this regrettable shortcoming, the castle looks what a castle should look like, and is worth a visit.

As Pierrefonds was a re-creation of the nouveau riche, *Le Vaux-le-Vicomte* was the real thing. This is a chateau which was designed to be shown off. This was no shrinking violet; this was something shouting "I am Here"! As you walk down from the stables and coach house towards the Chateau one is struck by the magnificent sense of proportion and symmetry the designer had in the Louis XIV period. Inside, there is a magnificent oval ceiling in *Le Salon des Muses*, painted in light blues, which is decorated to perfection rivaling that at the Residence in Wurzburg, Germany.. The gardens at Vicompte, designed by *La Nôtre*, are no ordinary gardens---they go on forever culminating in a lake, and are manicured to perfection. The creator of this beautiful Chateau, in 1661, was Nicolas Fouquet, the Finance Minister to Louis XIV, and by definition, a man of considerable means. He is said to have made the mistake of inviting the King down for the weekend to share in the beauty of his creation. Instead, the King was very suspicious of where the Minister got the money to build such an edifice, and aided and abetted by the minister's rivals, the King threw Fouquet into jail. All the craftsmen, masons, and artisans who built the Chateau were immediately packed off to Versailles where Louis wanted a bigger and better Chateau built. This included La Nôtre himself, who designed the gardens at Versailles. There must be a message here somewhere! Nevertheless, this was a favorite spot to bring visitors, but we discovered a hidden village nearby called *Bandy*, and it contained a small restaurant to which only the locals go, and whose Sunday lunch was a secret we kept to ourselves.

As you approach the town of Rambouillet from Maintenon, your first glimpse of the Chateau from the road is down a long avenue of trees called *Le Tapis Vert*. Rambouillet is just fifty kilometers from Paris, and this Chateau too sits serenely in its own park, a forest actually. The front is flanked by two towers with cone shaped roofs, which makes it look almost out of a fairy tale The large tower at the rear dates back to the 14th Century, but the main fabric is of Napoleon's time. The front faces an ornamental garden with large ponds, appropriately called *Le Jardin d'eau*. The Chateau has been used for many notable conferences and important negotiations, including Kissinger and Le Duc Tho on ending the Vietnam War, and more recently concerning the Bosnian issue. It is not hard to see why it is such an attractive venue.

So when one talks of Paris, one's mind must step out from the City to that rich heritage which lies beyond – but still nearby. You will be just as richly rewarded.

Bon Weekend!

23. Helga's first brush with Communism

When we grow up in the west, we naively assume that all reasonable people think and act as we do, have much the same values, and reach logical conclusions based on facts rather than ideology. It comes as a shock, therefore, when we run into situations we don't fully understand and cannot easily relate to. People dress much as we do, seem pleasant enough, but there is a certain, as the French say, "*je ne sais quoi* " We had heard all too much about communism during the course of the Cold War, but never quite understood why people who superficially lived like us could in fact be so different. So why was that?

We had an opportunity to explore this new, and totally unknown, avenue when we were invited to visit Yugoslavia. In short we were incredibly ignorant of what lay in store for us, and that is the fascination behind this story. It proved to be an indelible learning experience for both of us. At first, I was of two minds as to whether or not to accept the opportunity ; I was very busy, and didn't particularly want a week away. But the Yugoslavs kept pressing, and the offer and terms to include Helga were very attractive. The invitation was also a strange one; we were in fact invited , not by the central Yugoslav Government, but by one of two semi-antonymous province of Serbia, Voyvodina, the other being Kosovo. Serbia was one of the republics that made up the then Yugoslavia as a federation. Voyvodina lies about ninety kilometers north of the capital, Belgrade, and stretches as far as the Hungarian border to the north.

The republics that made up Yugoslavia in fact comprised separate ethnic groups, which continued to nurse old hatreds going back centuries, and with a passion which defies belief. These hatreds later fueled a massive civil war with bloodcurdling atrocities and a form of genocide couched in the ignominious euphemism of "ethnic cleansing". These disparate, and potentially warring factions, had been held together by the leadership of one remarkable man, Marshal Tito, who was a committed communist despite the fact that he had good relations with the western nations. In fact, Yugoslavia was an associate, not a full, member of the OECD. This was the reason that the invitation could be extended officially and accepted by me as Director of Research of the IEA. The invitation was to have discussions on energy research topics, and to give a speech. Nevertheless, at the time of our visit, the country was still firmly communist, the only one in the OECD.

It had been no mean feat on the part of Tito to keep the country from falling apart, and the western nations tacitly assumed that Tito's handiwork would outlive him, and that a free and unified nation would be his legacy. Today, sadly, we know otherwise. The events of the nineties are fresh in all our minds, with war crimes trials seemingly endless.

The person extending the invitation was a man called Otto Bene_. He was a Hungarian Jew by birth, but had managed to escape the opprobrium associated by that fact by being a close aide to Tito himself during Tito's guerilla warfare campaign against the Germans in Word War II. He proved too be a most accommodating and gracious host.

We flew from Paris to Belgrade in the tender mercies of JAT, Jugoslav Air Transport, the national airline. The interior was Spartan, to say the least, and the plane was full. The pilots came out from the terminal, and lumbered up the stairway carrying extra large containers, which they surreptitiously took with them into the cockpit. When we alighted, we went to passport control, and we were asked for our visa. Of course, we did not know we had to have such a thing, even though we were there at the invitation of the government. Naturally, visas could be purchased at the convenient booth next door, for a usurious fee of course. The pilots then appeared staggering under the load of their large bundles which turned out to be nothing other than plain old laundry detergent. Helga's education already extended to two important lesson in the space of five minutes; corruption was rampant, and that simple things like detergent were not available to the public in a communist society!

We drove the ninety kilometers to Novi Sad, the capital of Voyvodina. The Danube flows past an escarpment at this point, which divides the more mountainous country from the broad expanse of the immensely fertile Danubian Plain. Perched on the top of this escarpment is an imposing fairy tale fortress of the Maria-Theresa period called Petrovoydina. This was to be our home during our stay, and one could not have wished for a more imposing residence. Our hosts departed, and left us to settle in and have dinner. Helga noticed that the light bulb, should it have worked, was suspended precariously by two wires emerging from the ceiling. She mentioned this fact to me in the room, and surprise, surprise, it was fixed when we came back to our room from dinner. I had had a similar experience in a hotel room in Moscow, so I was prepared, but to Helga it was a distasteful revelation, and she had learned lesson number three; always assume that your conversations are being bugged in a communist country. From then on, we sallied forth to the promenade overlooking the Danube if we wanted to comment on anything confidential.

The next day was the start of work – hard work. We were to arrive at the first appointed meeting, one of an apparently endless stream, promptly at nine o'clock. We were then offered generous glasses of slivovitz. Helga and I were not accustomed to this form of introductory largesse, but learned lesson number four; accept, sip, but do not drink. Helga was a full participating member, and soon mastered the drinking protocol, particularly at nine in the morning. The topics ranged the gamut of energy problems, in which my hosts were both well informed, and had sound views. After a few of these meetings, on differing topics, the repetition of the approach meant that I was there for a purpose, namely to reinforce their own scientific views against the ideological edicts of the party bosses. In a communist state, party ideology trumps any logical action born of reason. Lesson number five, therefore, was; when wishing to appear polite, do not fall into the trap of agreeing with the preposterous.

The day ended in a sense of mounting fatigue. Dinner with our hosts was provided at one of the excellent restaurants, but we soon found that while there were delicious steaks in abundance to fill your plate, there were practically no vegetables other than potato. The reason was quite simp – it was still March, and there were as yet no fresh vegetables available in a centrally planned economy, even though they were in great profusion in nearby free market countries. Digesting such high protein fare, and at the same time doing our hosts the justice of their hospitality, provided an almost insuperable challenge to our digestive systems. Helga soon recognized the sixth lesson; eat enthusiastically but you're not expected to finish the meal. On the one day when we were left to our own devices for dinner, we went up to the promenade overlooking the Danube where there was a very respectable restaurant with a balalaika ensemble. After a week of eating excellent but large amounts of red meat, Helga was pleasantly surprised to find an attractive list of salads on the menu. However, her hopes were dashed when not a single salad out of the list of seven was actually available – communist society at its best! It transpired that the star turn, of national prominence, was a diminutive rotund man whose balalaika would have neatly fitted into his umbilicus. As we waited for the balalaika to finally disappear into his shirt, he strummed this minute instrument with even greater fervor, and even produced something approaching a recognizable tune. I was quite exhausted listening to the endless "ping-a-ping-a-ping", but Helga seemed to enjoy the music." *Chacun a son goût* "

We mercifully had a day free from interminable interviews and drove north across the Danubian Plain to a town called Suboti_a, just a few miles short of the Hungarian border. Voyvodina comprises distinct ethnic minorities, the largest of which is Hungarian. Their more genial disposition is in sharp contrast to that of the more taciturn Serbian population. On the way across the plain, we passed by large, and incredibly fertile, fields where the corn stubble was being burned; a practice frowned upon as wasteful by most modern agricultural authorities. We were told that Belgrade had tried to stop the practice but that the peasants would take no notice.. Suboti_a boasted a flourishing factory making electrical motors. It must have been one of the "crown jewels" for it to have been selected for our visit, so far out of our way. Helga had been warned by Otto Bene_ that it would not be a good idea to speak German because of lingering prejudices from World War II. To her surprise, German was fluently spoken by the Deputy Director, and she got more information from him than I did from the Director who spoke English!

The degree to which the local energy experts differed from the orthodoxy of the communist party became more apparent as the days went by. It culminated with a full ranging discussion with the national oil interests and the natural gas suppliers. The communist doctrine simply would not work, and it was no use going there to rubber stamp nonsense. I thought they were going to hug me! The final act of my visit to Novi Sad was a full scale lecture in a local auditorium with simultaneous translation. To our utter astonishment two hundred people showed up. I cannot proffer any opinion as to how it went down, but Helga gave me the appropriate reassurances later – did I ever need them!

The final act before our departure from Novi Sad next morning was a mandatory visit to the local party commissar. We tramped up an imposing stairway in a graceless official building- where we were received, it that be the word, by the great man himself. This flaccid, soulless individual with an expressionless face perfunctorily greeted us with the minimum of courtesy. Without more ado he then embarked upon his set party speech, which was as devoid of substance as it was packed with cliches strung together like so many sausages. We could not help noticing that he was about the first Serb we had met, quite unlike the mixture of Hungarians and Croats in the indigenous population of Novi Sad. Furthermore he was clearly an apparatchik from Belgrade placed in Novi Sad for ideological purposes only. It was Helga's first brush with communist polemics, and it was not a happy one. Lesson number seven, the longer a communist speaks, the less he has to say.

Leaving Novi Sad, we made our way back the ninety kilometers to Belgrade. We were no longer in Voyvodina; we were in Serbia – the contrast was dramatic, and only stone's throw away. Helga managed to get away for a few hours to explore the town, and I later felt that she had by far the better of the bargain. She managed to pick up a glorious crystal vase of immense size, and weight! By contrast, I had two interviews arranged for me that afternoon, but geniality and hospitality in Novi Sad had given way to, not exactly hostility, but studied indifference in Belgrade. Both interviews were with prestigious people, not party hacks, but the level of conversation and the focus on real energy issues of the day were desultory and a far cry from what they had been in Novi Sad. Interviews were polite, to be sure, but one felt they couldn't be over quick enough. What was happening? Simply put, what one did in Voyvodina was not in the slightest bit relevant in Serbia. Voyvodina was after all a province of Serbia, and didn't rate much attention. It was obvious then, and even more so today, that Serbia, as a nation rather than just another republic, felt that it was superior to any of the other parts of Yugoslavia. This impression was lasting with us, and has been born out tragically by subsequent events. Helga and I saw what was happening, but did not understand either the implications well enough or the intensity of the deep seated prejudices and feelings. Lesson eight was that we saw that Yugoslavia was ready to fly apart, but we did not foresee its ferocity.

Our hosts kindly arranged for a short vacation as a "reward" for our visit, and flew us next day to Dubrovnik, on the Adriatic coast of Croatia. This was a remarkably generous gesture, and much appreciated by us. Dubrovnik is a priceless gem, with its old walled city. Its walls drop like cliffs into the sea, and walking around them, with constant changes in level, can be exhilarating but quite exhausting. To think that the Serbs would later wantonly bombard this precious jewel of the past, causing serious damage, is beyond comprehension not to speak of the crass stupidity. We stayed for two nights in a hotel situated at the bottom of a corniche, and with a splendid view of the red roofed ancient town across a narrow stretch of water. It was a fitting conclusion toa well worth while and insightful trip.

On coming home to Paris, I was eager to discuss my findings with the Yugoslav representative to the OECD. I wrote a fairly comprehensive report, and invited the gentleman to lunch. I made the suggestion that we might organize some young Yugoslav graduate students to make stays in IEA countries to learn up-to-date energy technology directly. The lunch was convivial enough, as are most French lunches, but my companion was totally disinterested and to my dismay, but not to my complete surprise, I heard nothing further of the matter again. It was if our visit had never taken place. On the positive side, Helga and I felt we had learned a very great deal in a very short time, but we wished later we had been able to read the "tea leaves" more clearly in the view of subsequent events. That they were there to be read, there is no doubt, but just couldn't look below the surface to see them

24. Bumbling............into Wine-Speak.

A lesson for neophytes

Many airlines encourage you to take away the house magazine when you leave the aircraft. It is usually full of articles written for a five year old, and with advertisements that offer articles with no conceivable use. It came as a pleasant surprise, therefore, that on leaving the Air France Concorde passengers are invited to take away a handsome copy of Hugh Johnson's Pocket Guide to Wines. My ignorance about wines at that time was overpowering, and twenty years later some might question whether there had been any improvement.. Nevertheless, the Pocket Guide provided at least a start.

It is fair to say, then, that Helga and I in the Spring of 1981, could not be counted among the world's wine savants. Some friends of ours have aspired to be *Chevaliers of the This or That Tasse de Vin* –   but for us wines could be defined as being either red, white, or pink. We suspected that the pink was merely a crafty mixture of the first two, so we discounted pink. Our next discovery, from the little book, was that, in France, wines of particular quality are grown in three principal areas, the Bordeaux, the Bourgogne, and the Rhone Valley. On further reading it transpired that they are also grown on nearly every square inch of France in between. The "Little Book" is very emphatic about France and its relationship to wine. It says, "France makes every kind of wine, and invented most of them". Whow! That's quite a claim. But it goes on to say that " Her wine trade, both exporting and importing, dwarfs that of any other country". Not just bigger – it dwarfs all others! Helga feels that this claim is flagrant nonsense---try to buy a bottle of California wine in any Paris store ! This whopper notwithstanding, it was obvious that if wine was indeed a second religion in France, we just couldn't sit out five years here in our present state of agnosticism !

In America, in the sixties and seventies, most people accepted that wine came in either bottles, or in gallon jugs if you were having a party! What every French kid knows from the cradle, of course, is that wine coming from Bordeaux comes in a different shaped bottle than wine coming from Burgundy. He also probably learns, before even his ABC and probably as a catechism on his first day at *l'école maternelle*, the fascinating statistic that one vine usually produces about one bottle of wine a year. Not having been weaned on wine-speak, we clearly had some ground to make up! It was at this point that Helga had her brain wave – let us go to the *Foire de Paris*, and find out a bit more!

She had read about it in *Le Figaro* during the week, and she thoughtfully cut out the directions on how to get there. We were advised to take the *Peripherique* as far as the *Balard* Exit, which we did. There, we joined a slow procession on one of three roads converging on just one entrance to a vast parking lot formed from a demolished industrial site. Shuttle busses were waiting to take us to the entrance to the Fair which was now a goodly walk away. So an hour and a half after leaving home we were at last inside. This will show you what neophytes in Paris we were – on returning later in the afternoon we exited the car park to find ourselves only a few yards from a bridge, Pont Garigliano, crossing the *Seine* next to our home Quartier! We could have walked there in less than twenty minutes, and the PC Bus would have done it in ten! We had completed four-fifths of a circle when we had parked the car!

The Fair was designed to introduce the burgeoning French middle class to the delights of investing their new found prosperity into their homes – or their second homes! Fully built country cottages were on display, complete with every good thing one would want to stuff into them. They were rather nicely designed homes, but our short visit to Normandy had convinced us that the same design could become awfully boring when replicated in their hundreds in villages along the coast ! The "furnishings" area caught our eye, and the rug merchants were in their usual feeding frenzy. We were in need of a carpet in the hallway of the apartment, and we spotted a rather interesting five-kneeler prayer rug at a price which, years later, I would still consider exorbitant. It had a rather pleasant sheen on it when we bought it, but my later experience with Parisian rug merchants leads me to the cynical belief that the sheen came from a spray can, rather than the oil of the native wool. However, we still like it, and it serves to remind us of that day when the two rookies came to town! The only other exhibit of lasting note was that of *La Maison de Biblioteque.* They specialized in an excellent selection of library bookcases, and after visiting their showroom in the 14th Arrondissment we purchased the first of the eight bookcases which line my Study walls today.

The fairground site was divided in two by the Peripherique, and one had to cross a bridge to gain access to the second part. Despite colorful banners and bunting, nothing could disguise the downright ugliness of the huge and ungainly brick warehouse structure which dominated the site. But inside, it was another world, dedicated to the God Bacchus. It seemed so large that it was almost impossible to see one end from the other. It was crammed with the stalls of wine sellers from all over the country, each with his open bottles and small cups calling on you to sample their wares. How to avoid getting smashed just going down one aisle was a problem in itself! To give the lie to the claim of the French being big importers of wine as well as exporters, there was one lone German tending his solitary stand – so we bought a case from him. Our Two Rookies were totally at a loss to distinguish between the merits of wine from one French wine growing area over another, so there was nothing left but to give them a try. Gathering up our courage, we resolved to sin bravely. It was extraordinary how much easier it got as we made our way down the aisle. I am not sure we ever made it to the far end!

On the way we came on a stall which said *"Brevard Père et Fils, Chateau-Neuf du Pape".* This name rang a vague bell, so we decided to -- just take a sip.. Not really knowing what a good wine should taste like, we were rather cautious. The voluble and suitably rustic proprietor, displaying an encyclopedic knowledge of wines with great authority, persuaded us that this wine would be a smash hit in about five years. Five Years! We normally bought wine during the day for dinner that same night! Nevertheless, we bought a case of his 1978 vintage, He also had acreage in the *Gigondas* area which, while not maybe up to Chateau-Neuf standards, the "Little Red Book" spoke of it as a "worthy neighbor". (Do I detect a touch of "damning with faint praise"?). So why not, let's have a case of that too. "Helga!", I cried, "We've just bought thirty-six bottles of wine at one go -- we've never bought more than four before"! When the time finally came for us to leave Paris in July of1985, we were to ship four-hundred and fifty bottles back with us with our household goods! As a postscript to our Foire purchase, when we actually came to pay a call on *Brevard, Père et Fils* at their home address a couple of years later, we found a rather run down establishment, closed for summer vacations, which was a fair distance both from the village of *Chateau-Neuf du Pape* <u>and</u> its surrounding vineyards. Humph!

In retrospect, the vintners exhibiting at the *Foire de Paris* offer some good wines, to be sure, but not generally of the first rank. And for a very good reason – the first rank has no need to sell its wines through that outlet because their reputations have for years sold their products for them, and they find a ready market through well established channels. The *Foire de Paris* offers the more bourgeois vintners the opportunity to expose their products to a wider clientele, and of course get subsequent mailing lists. For Helga and me, it was "Wine Sampling 101", and although it was impossible to take it all in, it was a great education and not a little fun too. There was one lesson to take away – there are fine wines to be had in the less expensive range, and this brings us to our next discovery, our friend *Chaumvermeille*, a *negoçiant* from *Bordeaux* .

Leslie Boxer had been at the IEA quite a few years by this time, and was married to a very elegant French lady, Colette. Leslie was already well versed in the ways of the wine world as it pertained to getting value for money. He had discovered this *negoçiant* in Bordeaux who shipped bulk wine from the surrounding prime wine growing areas. It is still a mystery how this is done, but wine can only be produced from a given area, say St. Emillion, up to a prescribed quota. Above that quota, surplus wine is collected by a *negoçiant,* such as *Chaumvermeille,* and marketed as non-Chateau bottled wine but still bearing the *Appellation Controlée* of the region. *Appellation Controlée* is the seal of authenticity, as it were, of the region of origin and the quality that it implies. *Chaumvermeille* would send you a "cubitainer" of thirty-three litres of wine in a tough plastic bag surrounded by a protective cardboard box. This would be enough to fill about forty-four 75ml bottles. By this method, one could buy plain Bordeaux Superieur for about a dollar-fifty, and a good St Emilion or a Pommerol for about two-fifty. The negociant would also send you the appropriate labels, and sufficient corks. This do-it-yourself approach to wine purchasing had considerable attraction, both for the pocket and the palate, and led to bucolic celebrations known as "bottling parties". among fellow Americans

Preparations for a bottling party start well in advance – bottles have to be accumulated. After all, you don't want to be the only one showing up with a derisory five bottles! The process of accumulating enough bottles proved to be disturbingly easy. The bottles are put in the bath, with lots of very hot water. Bordeaux bottles and Burgundy bottles were co-mingled, because in truth few of us appreciated the difference at the time. The hot bath not only removes the old labels, but serves to loosen up some of the less than appealing crud that remains in the bottle when you thought you had emptied it! Leslie Boxer, had a corking machine, and for providing this service he got two free bottles. So just before the appointed day, the railroad delivered three cubitainers of wine to our door. They weigh a ton – well seventy pounds each anyway. Now we are all set !.

On "bottling day", each armed with his quota of empty bottles, a remarkably sober gathering gets down to the serious work before them. Labels are stuck on to the bottles using milk as the adhesive. Quality control on this procedure is tight, for it is thought that squiffy labels do not speak well for the contents of the bottle. For practical reasons, this requirement was relaxed as the day wore on, and as the contents of the bottles were monitored by scientifically based sampling at appropriate intervals!. Their mission accomplished, the merry warriors gather their share of the loot, and try to squeeze them into their non-elastic cars. A good and profitable day is declared by all, although it is interesting how the intervals between bottling parties got shorter and shorter, either because of their popularity or because supplies ran out too fast.

After being indoctrinated into the wines of Bordeaux by *Chaumvermeille*, albeit at a fairly primitive level, the Region became a "must" to visit. And so Helga and I traveled the six hundred kilometers to the quaint town of St Emilion; at least we had a fleeting acquaintance with the name from the labels we had slapped on bottles! Hugh Johnson's Pocket Wine Guide, by now our wine Bible, rates the wines of St Emilion among the finest anywhere and their *Grand Cru Classé*, like *Le Cheval Blanc*, par excellence. We picked the chateau of *Cadet Piola* for a visit simply because we had met the owner in town, and we spent some time in his *caves* learning the gentle art of *dégustation*, which is by no means as disgusting as the name sounds – it merely means "tasting". We were surprised to find that their *caves* literally were caves, dank, dark, and dismal. We added a few cases of *Corbin-Michotte* "78 to the trunk on a visit to another chateau. Some bottles lasted nearly twenty years with enduring quality.

We picked a well situated hotel in town from the Michelin Guide called *L'Auberge de la Commanderie*, with a bedroom heavily decorated in red velvet. The most pleasant ambiance was offset to some extent by the daughter of the owners, who proved to be an incorrigibly irascible individual. She obviously resented doing much of the work of an owner without being one, an attitude she was not shy in sharing with the world. As we were loading up our car with suitcases outside the front door upon our departure she indicated that we were an annoyance because loading outside the front door was only for her. As she so delicately put it, *"je travail ici – je ne suis pas en vacances"*. Sometimes the French attitude to customers could be described as thinly veiled toleration, at best.

We were to learn that the worldwide reputation of a wine was often in contradistinction to the sophistication of the village that bears its name. When we visited *St Estèphe* at the tip of the *Médoc*, it was a hot day, and it was lunchtime – here we were in a village whose name is renowned the world over for its excellent wines, and what better than to savor those wines over a pleasant lunch. We were puzzled that we couldn't find any obvious eating place so we enquired of a woman pushing a pram in an otherwise empty street. "Oh no." she said, somewhat apologetically," we are not blessed with such luxuries in *St Estèphe*". In a word, as far as the village of *St Estèphe* was concerned "there was no there there" – it was a respected name on a wine bottle, and no more. Likewise, the village of *Pommerol*, next door to *St Emelion*, was also not "blessed" with a restaurant despite its wine, but boasted nevertheless a very fine church!

On the other side of the country, bordering the River *Saône,* are the vineyards of the Burgundy Region. These are on the whole lighter wines than the Bordeaux; they range from the much sought-after wines of the Côte D'Or, south of Dijon, to the wines of the Beaujolais area to the west of Mâcon. We were coming back to Paris from the Haute Savoie one Sunday morning, having managed to get through Lyon very early before it choked itself to a standstill. We had some time to spare as we drove up the rather uninteresting Autoroute, and decided to have a look at *Mâcon*. I don't know exactly why we did that, since *Mâcon* doesn't even merit even a humble star in the Guide Michelin. The Michelin does not give stars for drabness, but if it did it would have awarded at least two; obviously it was certainly nothing to write home about. But on looking through the slender (two line) list of attractions I came across a reference to *La Maison Mâconaise des Vins*. It turned out to be yet another unprepossessing building facing the river, with a long flight of steps going up to the imposing double front doors. Since a notice indicated a restaurant, and since it was approaching midday, we thought this might be as reasonable a place as any in town to have lunch. Clambering up the steps, we found ourselves in a bare hall containing even barer scrubbed tables – and we were the only ones around. Someone appeared at last, and graciously informed us that it was a wine cooperative, and sold wine from the regional vineyards around *Mâcon* much in the same way *Chaumvermeille* had done in *Bordeaux*, ie with a full *Appellation Controlée* but with no "*domaine*" vineyard ascribed to it. A sampling, with decent size glasses, proved them excellent, and we were soon in the process of buying a few cases. The selection ran the gamut of wines from the *Beaujolais*, through *Mercurey, St Veran, Mâcon Villages, Côtes de Beaune, and Rully.* The prices were inexpensive, and the quality proved uniformly good -- we unexpectedly had a "find".. We were to buy there with confidence again a few times later, and even brought some back to America with us.

We asked if they were serving lunch, and they said "yes" they were, although they were expecting quite a crowd, it being Sunday. We were still the only ones there, so with our dog "Putzi" we sat at the far end of one of the tables feeling very alone and a bit foolish. In no time at all, busses outside discharged what seemed like a large proportion of the surrounding countryside! Clearly, the locals liked the place, so we felt encouraged The meal was a set menu -- it was unquestionably the worst meal we were to be offered during our entire time in France. It consisted of huge steamed potatoes, which they gratuitously called "*Pommes de Terre Anglais au Vapeur*", and Tripe sausage, with huge chunks of the stuff, not even ground, inside a skin as thick as an inner tube . We took one bite, and that was enough. Putzi, on the other hand had a grand time, and had never had so much food shoveled down to her before – or after, come to that!

In later years, and on other expeditions, we expanded our knowledge to include some very interesting places, Domaines, and Chateaux, but we were very glad to have got the opportunity to get access to a good selection of quality wines from a variety of regions at relatively modest prices. By the end of the summer, Helga and I had climbed, just a little, up the still steep learning curve!

25. A Summer Pot-pourri.

Did you ever think when September comes around – where did the summer go? This has puzzled me all my life. In England, the answer was easy -- it never came. Whenever we have a rare nasty day here in Washington in late October, when it is perhaps cold and drizzly, I refer to it as "Good English Boy Scouts Camping Weather". In Washington, we spend most of July and August counting the days till September arrives, when the mercury once more retreats below ninety degrees and you don't feel that you are soaked to the skin in perspiration. (I was taught in that quaint English way that horses "sweat" and gentlemen "perspire"!). One waters the flowers outside in the garden in Washington constantly on the remote chance that you might venture out from your air conditioning long enough to see them ! Summer in Paris, 1981, was memorable only because one wondered when it would stop raining ! Otherwise, it came and went without any one really noticing its presence, except that the long evenings are always a delight.

To illustrate the point, Monika made her first trip to Paris in July, and we felt it would be good for her if we were to take for a quick trip to Switzerland. We stopped first in Weggis, on Lake Luzern, where it was cool but did not rain. We then went over the Susten Pass to the Bernese Oberland, where not only did it rain but it snowed – heavily. We had planned to go over the mountains to the Zermatt area, but the passes were cut off, and communications inside Switzerland came to a

Eric H. Willis

standstill. So we beat a hasty and forlorn retreat back to Paris---at least we could enjoy the same the rain for free! I am sure Monika rated the trip a success, but we had hoped for better things.

Summer heralds the end of the Season, as far as diplomatic affairs are concerned. Delegations go on home leave to be chastised by bureaucrats for being too lax with the "Natives". Actually, only the foolish do that, because the crafty want to be kept in your good graces so that they can be fêted with good French dinners when they come to Paris. When you return, it is a different story! Before the resident diplomatic population leaves Paris, there are End of Season Meetings which strangely coincide with End of Season Receptions. The best of these, by far, was that put on by the Japanese at their Ambassador's Residence in Neuilly. Ambassador Myasaki was a diminutive man, probably no more than five feet tall, with a mousetrap mind. He was also the Chairman of the IEA Governing Board at the time. The buffet is lavish, and waiters behind side tables prepare fresh sushi, tempura, and teriyaki offerings that melt in your mouth.

At the other end of the diplomatic scale comes the Reception of those pillars of Parisian official life, Eric and Helga. We had to wrack our brains as to how to address the invitation. We came up with:

"Helga, and Eric Willis cordially invite you to a Reception in their Home.....", and the following year we just dropped the comma! Neat trick!

This was a good story that I have treasured and retold often for twenty years. There was only one thing wrong with it – it turns out not to be true ! I have just unearthed the original invitations for both years, and find that the 1981 invitation merely said:

"Helga and I would like to invite you to a cocktail party....".

Not so imaginative, but it achieved the objective without revealing our, then, marital status!

France's special day is Bastille Day, July 14th. It is a public holiday, naturally, and is the occasion for a very elaborate parade down the Champs Elysees to the Place de la Concorde where it is reviewed by the President of the Republic with bands playing and flags waving. The is an overflight by the French Air Force at the climax of the event with a Tricolor of red white and blue smoke trailing behind them. The Glory of France is celebrated, and the population justifiably "feels good:" about their country. Although we were quite a step from the Champs Elysees, it turned out that we were not going to miss a good portion of it. We decided that, being a holiday, we would take the opportunity to get up late for a leisurely breakfast. You can imagine our consternation when at about seven we awoke to hear an overwhelming occupation force of tanks, armored personnel carriers, and nuclear tipped mobile rocket launchers thundering along the canyon below our bedroom window. They were proceeding from their staging areas beyond St Cloud to the get in line for the Parade. They were quite a sight, better so without any enemy insignia on them!

Just after Bastille Day, I had to go to Almeria, Spain for the inaugural ceremony of our IEA collaborative project on Solar Energy. It was a major investment, and the participating countries were very enthusiastic about it. The trip turned out to be a professional triumph and a bit of a personal disaster ! Wally Hopkins and I decided to go together, and we very pretty rushed as we went for the plane at Orly Airport. We got Air France's Classe d'Affaires, which meant you sat in the front of the plane on cherry red seats instead of the Air France standard blue. We just made it – they literally closed the door behind us. Breathing a sigh of relief, we took our appointed seats. It soon became obvious that something was wrong — there was a nasty smell,. We were taxiing by this time, and as I tried to get up from my seat, the fight attendant shouted "Monsieur, ne bouge pas!". Yes Ma'am ! As I sat down again, I was aware that my backside was well---wet! When airborne, I complained bitterly to the attendant, who gave me another seat. I filed a complaint, since it appeared that the plane had just arrived from North Africa prior to our departure, and it was not unusual for there to be wet seats ! Air France subsequently gave me a voucher for four thousand francs as compensation for a ruined suit.

We changed planes in Madrid, and took a second plane on Iberia to Almeria on the Mediterranean. By now I had dried out, but on arriving at the hotel and changing, the cherry red of the seat had penetrated all my clothing, and my backside was something akin to a rangatan.

The solar electric site had an intriguing mix of large scale experiments on harnessing the sun's rays to generate electricity. By having the experiments in one location, it was possible to make valid comparisons of technologies. There was a "power tower', in which a field of a hundred mirrors focused the sun's rays on a "solar furnace" at the top of the tower. The other experiments used ground based collectors of two different designs. I remained somewhat concerned about the heat transfer technology on the solar power tower. They had elected to install a technology developed for the nuclear breeder reactor which entailed a liquid sodium loop. Inside a well controlled environment with technologists who understood these things it was fine, but out here in the "field" I was concerned lest we might have bitten off a bit more than we could chew. Liquid sodium on the loose was not a good thing to have around---it is nasty stuff. While experiments are, by definition , permitted to fail, I did not want this one to be in that category. It gave me more confidence, the project was well managed, successful, and certainly something we could be proud of.

Unfortunately, my personal embarrassments were not at an end, for at lunch, in my own way which Helga will attest to, I dribbled soup down my new silk tie. At dinner, the soup was on the table as we came to it. We all stood before our chairs while an invocation was given As we all sat down my tie swung merrily forward and, in slow motion, performed a ritual act of total immersion in the soup. There are some guys you can't take anywhere!

Monika was due to go back home, at the end of July, so I accompanied her back to Washington. Through a sympathetic flight attendant I managed to get her a seat in Business Class. It was better than that provided by Air France on the way to Madrid, but not by much. Believe it or not, when Business Class was first introduced it meant almost nothing except paying more – the extra amenities were minimal, and TWA folded down the center seat of a row of three. But Monika was nevertheless thrilled at the "one-up-man-ship", which is what it was 75% about anyway – "think of all those poor devils BACK THERE!". I had some business to attend to at the Department of Energy, still under sentence of extinction, but appearing alive and well nevertheless. It was there that I first encountered the cult of the "Jelly Bean". It seemed that our good President Ronnie Reagan was addicted to jelly beans. They resided on his desk, from whence he would extract a handful as the fancy took him. This quite innocent foible on his part was extrapolated to the level of a solemn sacrament by those persons who had contributed sufficient campaign money as to warrant some patronage in the form of a Presidential Appointment. I did not pay much attention at the first one, but by the time I met the third of the DOE Assistant Secretaries I was convinced that a glass jar of Jelly Beans was part of the standard office equipment issue, together with paper, pens and pencils. The second thing that struck me was that they had very little inklng of why they were there except to wrap up the Department, denigrate international organizations, and to extol the virtues of the market place *uber alles* . Why anyone would wish to undertake a job scheduled to be abolished in short order was beyond my comprehension. The truly wise ones were like my friend Don Kerr, sitting it out and being immensely productive in Los Alamos.

I had some legal business of my own to attend to during the week in Washington, and I left with the path now clear to my marrying Helga in September. I first had to observe a time honored tradition ---I had to ask her Mother for her Daughter's hand in marriage! Hertha was a bit nonplused at first, but soon entered into the spirit of my call: she was also very gracious in giving her enthusiastic consent. The paper work was thought to take a month for it to go through the mill. We had ruled out getting married in France because the number of notarized documents, each translated into French and again notarized, would have done a phone book justice. England was the next obvious choice; we spoke the language and my Family was there. So a few days in England in early August were an important prelude to making firm arrangements. I thought I might take the opportunity to introduce

Helga to Cambridge, where I spent twelve happy years, and for which I have great affection.

Cambridge University is properly renowned the world over, but the visitor is less entranced with its academic prowess than the sheer attractiveness of the place, with architecture spanning the best part of a thousand years. My own College, Clare was founded in 1324. One of the attractions is the River Cam, which wends its leisurely way through lawns and gardens behind some of the old College buildings, and is thus known as the "Backs". The preferred mode of transport on the Cam is the Punt. A punt is a flat bottomed boat, about twenty feet long, developed for crossing shallow water through a fair amount of standing reeds. It looks deceptively easy; all you have to do is to propel it along using the fourteen foot pole that the boatman thoughtfully hands to you with a twinkle in his eye. The pole has a metal piece on the end, the shape of the letter "C, which ensures traction in the mud.. No re-blooded male can reject the challenge from this old codger with such a disarming smile. The "punter" stands on a wooden platform at the rear and by dropping the pole into the water, pushes the punt, and its contents of adoring women, along for a pleasant outing on the River. Well, it can work that way – but often not the first time. There are numerous low bridges along the river, which provide the punter with the challenge of an aquatic steeplechase – there is no way an upright pole will go through, nor can he if he stands up straight. The first rule of punting is "Never hold on to the pole!!". This is counterintuitive, because no-one wants to give up his only means of propulsion. Sooner or later, the novice punter gets his pole stuck hard in the mud. Gleeful watchers on the bridges are rewarded at the sight of some poor soul manfully clutching onto his pole as the punt remorselessly slides away from under him. Then, in slow motion, the pole disengages itself from the mud at the bottom, and to everyone's applause he gracefully descends on the falling pole into the murky waters of the Cam. I will not use this opportunity to give you a tutorial for successful punting---just go and try for yourself sometime!

Another visit was an important hurdle to get over, and was a "must". Nigel's maternal Grandmother and Grandfather, Jean and Alan, lived about twenty miles north of London. Their daughter, my dear wife Renee, had died in 1972, and Jean had helped us get through this heart wrenching ordeal more or less intact – I will be forever in her debt. I include the visit in this narrative because it is also a testament to Helga's sheer personality and sincerity in pulling it off. Here she was, being introduced as someone who was, perhaps, going to steal their son-in-law away from them. Suffice to say that Helga established her own warm relationship with both of them until Jean passed away at the age of ninety three, Alan preceding her ten years previously. Her other two children, Peter and Myrna, and their spouses, Lucy and Nigel (number two, as my son Nigel likes to say) continue this remarkable and solid family friendship. It is a source of my continued gratitude to Helga for her graciousness, and to them for their understanding, that this has remained such a warm relationship.

The next stop was to meet up with my Mother in Pound Hill, near Crawley. My sister Doreen had had some contact with a local church which seemed to posess some very enlightened views concerning their care for old people. It was Christ Church, of the United Reformed Church, in Crawley, England. The Minister was a Rev Alan Greene, and when my Sister mentioned that she had a Mother would benefit from more social interaction with her peers, he was enthusiastic about her joining the group of Seniors who had lunch there once a week. Win was somewhat reticent and, since Helga and I happened to be there at the time. Helga offered to take her along on her first luncheon visit. Helga recalls that Win was like a frightened rabbit, and it was with some difficulty that she persuaded Win to give it a try. Try she did, and liked it, although she was somewhat critical of being bunched up with some of those "old fogies", as if she herself was any spring chicken. Thus when the subject of our impending marriage came up, the Christ Church Crawley and its enlightened Minister immediately both came to the fore. This was particularly true since the Church of England church that Mother attended had turned us down flat on the grounds that we were both divorcees, and were therefore quite unworthy. What they would say today now that the Heir to the British Throne is a divorcee, and wants to marry another divorcee, is an interesting and not yet solved question. His Mother, the Queen of England, is of course the Head of the Established Church. Tough luck fella'---I am not sure what Mummy will say ! So Christ Church was the unequivocal venue of choice for us lesser folk – if they were willing, that is.

The Rev Alan Greene turned out to be very straight forward fellow, with whom it was easy to talk with complete frankness, We met him at his office, next to the Church, and told him why it was that two middle aged American divorcees living in Paris would want him to marry them in Crawley, England. I am sure he hears lots of stories, but I wouldn't think he hears that one too often. To begin with, Helga and I wanted to get married in a church rather than in a civil ceremony, and that we wanted our family around us as we did so. We told him that four would be flying in from America for the ceremony; Helga's Mother, Hertha, and our three children, and that we wanted our three children particularly to be the witnesses – they were the next generation, and we wanted them to have confidence in our future. Rev Greene really wanted to assure himself that this was not another lost cause, for he had had a few disappointments and did not want to feel he was officiating at yet another fragile marriage. We could not help but sympathize with his point of view, but we felt strongly that this would not be the case. He consented, and we tentatively arranged for September 16th to be the appointed date. All we had to do now was to ensure the paper trail kept in step with our timetable. This was largely out of our hands, since our fate rested probably in the hands of some law clerk in Fairfax, Virginia. We would just have to be patient –   to a point!

26. Discovering the Haute Savoie

South of Lake Geneva, there is an Alpine area of France known as the Haute Savoie. Among many high peaks it contains the highest in Europe, Mont Blanc. This seemed an appropriate "get-away" for a few weeks while the legal wheels in Washington ground their way forward with glacial speed towards producing our papers. This was fresh territory for us, so we sought a center from which we could explore. It had to be in the midst of the mountains, near the *La Chaine d'Aravis*. Careful scrutiny of the map showed that *La Clusaz* was just about right, so we booked at a hotel there for three initial nights. Unfortunately, we were thoroughly underwhelmed when we arrived after the nearly six hundred kilometer drive from Paris. This was not because of the scenery, which was truly magnificent all around, but because the town had absolutely no soul. A conveniently situated small village, with a residual core of old world houses, had been set upon by developers dedicated to providing the maximum accommodation for the ski season. As a result, most houses and chalets were unoccupied, gray and stark, totally devoid of flowers, drapes, or other signs that human beings might inhabit them sometime. It was, in summer, a ghost town. Nevertheless, it was a good starting point to find something better, and the very next day we were to be most pleasantly surprised by what we found. It was a village, still with its old word charm intact, in an adjoining valley with a line of jagged peaks of the Aravis Chain on one flank . We fell in love with it, and moved there after three days. It was called *Le Grand Bornand*, and it was to give us much pleasure, not only over the coming weeks, but in three successive winters for the skiing.

L'Aiguille de Midi is a dramatic sight, although you have to crane your neck to see it from the valley floor. As the name suggests it stands, stark and gaunt, and ten thousand feet tall like a sharp needle above the town of *Chamonix..* It can be reached by a series of cable cars which ascend the bare and steep cliff face to the summit. At the summit, a great adventure awaits you. Imagine yourself, for a minute, two double seats facing each other and surrounded by nothing more than a fibre glass cabin with windows. The cabin is suspended by an arm which grabs onto a moving cable. Three such cabins are grouped together, and the three are released as a unit onto the moving cable. What follows is breath taking. The cable crosses the great expanse of the *La Valée Blanche,* with its crevasses like open jaws waiting to consume any morsels that may come their way. They unfortunately did on one occasion when a French Mirage fighter cut one of the cables, but now was not the time to think about that ! Passing under the daunting summit of *Mont Blanc,* one reaches a transfer station where one proceeds in a new set of cabins until, surprise, one finds onself in – Italy! How did we get here? No matter, no sooner were we off the cable cars than we had to get in line for more than an hour to get one back. That was Italy, that was!

Helga and I were reasonable hikers in those days, and we look at some of the photographs in utter astonishment at these two intrepid mountaineers playing rock apes -- could they have been us?. One particularly challenging hike started from a pass called *Le Col de la Colombière,* which entailed climbing the rocky path for seven hundred meters to the *Pointe de Balafrasse.* As we climbed, we noticed *Mont Blanc* peeping above the peaks of the Aravis Chain. But it was fascinating to watch *Mont Blanc* grow and grow as we climbed further – when we reached the summit its beautiful silhouette filled the skyline. I bought some hiking "togs" in *Grand Bornand*: a stout pair of hiking boots and a pair of French short Shorts. The hiking boots still do yeoman service on the trails at Wintergreen, but the short shorts were banned by Helga as not befitting a man whose age is beyond the point where he can display that much thigh!

A tour of the area revealed a contrasting range of scenery, from lush forest to almost semi-arid mountainsides. Annecy was one of the major towns of the region at the head of a lake of that name. It was there that we were introduced to the new fashion of topless bathing beaches on the shore of the lake. There were no shortage of shapes and sizes on which to gaze. It has to be said that there were some very shapely breasts on display, but for the most part the spectacle served as a reminder that the humble "bra" was not invented for nothing. We took the car up the *Semnoz* Mountains where we had an unexpectedly fine lunch at a rundown hotel with great views of the lake, and the town of *Talloires* on its shoreline. *Talloires* was renowned both for its elegance and for being especially hospitable to notorious deposed despots. It sported a hotel, the three star *Auberge du Père Bise;* Helga, with her usual flair, marched in to ask the prices. She came out armed with brochures and a price list containing sums rivaling the National Debt. Unfortunately the present despot in residence was just a mere former Central American Dictator: business was obviously not what they were accustomed to.

The Grand Bornand Valley rises steeply as it reaches the mountains, and there are a number of attractive farmhouses around the meadows of the River Borne. We saw a very neat notice on the gate of one of them, which simply said

"Tomme
Reblochon"

It was a prosperous looking farm, and obviously the farmer was proud to display his name on it, as any of us would have been. We congratulated Tomme Reblochon on keeping such a neat and flourishing property, and walked on up the steep end of the valley. On the way, we saw another farm, much less elegant than the first one, also marked Tomme Reblochon on a less fancy sign. We concluded that Tomme also owned this farm too, but that it was not his main one. On the way up we passed by slopes of *myrtiles*, or blueberry bushes. A family was at work gathering the fruit. They had wide box shaped flat wooden scoops; the scoops had metal tines protruding from the base of the box like a big comb. The idea was to thrust the scoop through the *myrtile* bushes and scoop up the blueberries with the comb. We found later they they fetched a good price in the market.

After climbing about another fifteen hundred feet, we stopped and ate our lunch near a rather primitive mountain farmhouse at *Plattuy* with an adjoining cowshed. I decided I would like to explore further, and followed up the path which eventually would lead to the top of one of the peaks. I had overestimated my training for this adventure despite my daily jogging in Paris; I decided that another few thousand feet to the top was not for me today! I descended by the same tortuous path, and rejoined Helga near the farmhouse. She was now carrying a small package. It appears that a young woman had appeared from the farm and was going into the cowshed. Helga also noticed an even more decrepit sign on which you could just make out the words "Tomme Reblochon". The woman waved to Helga as she passed, and Helga must have used the word Reblochon as part of her greeting. The woman smiled and enthusiastically motioned to Helga to follow her into the dairy of the cowshed. There she found that "Tomme" was <u>actually a cheese</u>, as was "Reblochon". There was nothing to it but to buy the proffered cheese, which was now in her package. Well, even us dumb ones can learn something!!

Not all hikes have such nice endings – this one nearly ended in a divorce before the marriage---at least this would be a first. The weather had been threatening all morning, but looked like clearing up. Never one to stand around waiting for something to happen, I suggested that we take the *telephèrique* from *La Clusaz* to a high point, I am sure beloved of skiers eloquently called *L'Etoile des Veiges*, and walk down again through the forest. So, with Putzi in tow as always, we ascended to the top. As you might imagine, the view was stunning! The map showed a delightful walk, all downhill, back to *La Clusaz*. Indeed it was all downhill after that! After about ten minutes, when it was too late to climb back up again, the Heavens opened. The ensuing Pluvial would be a candidate for the Guinness Book of Records. I cannot begin to describe the state of the three miserable creatures who struggled to avoid the incessant new streams which poured forth from the mountain top, let alone that which was descending from the sky by the bucket. Those fifteen hundred feet must be the longest we have ever descended, and seemed to take for ever! Three drenched, barely surviving, creatures got back to the hotel, had hot baths, and didn't emerge again that day ! Putzi went on the bed, and I---to the Dog House!

Geneva was about fifty miles from Grand Bornand, and for some reason or other, which I now cannot recall, I had to meet someone at the US Embassy. He couldn't meet me in Paris, but for some reason he could meet me in Geneva. I had been a frequent visitor to the Mission in the early seventies when it was located in the Rue de Lausanne, and when I was attending the Geneva Disarmament Talks. But they outgrew it and besides, the security was horrible. They now had a spanking new fortress on the hill outside town. Helga, meanwhile was content to be left to her own devices in what was anyway a wonderful town to "mooch" about. When I got back I met her having tea outside the Hotel de Rhone. She was quite excited, and announced that she had been to a Jewelers in Old Town, and had found the <u>very</u> Wedding Ring she wanted. If Helga was happy, that was just fine. With the Wedding only a month away, it seemed not too soon to buy this essential article for the ceremony. After a very nice dinner, that Old Town Geneva excels in, we went to the Jewelers in question. The ring was, if I my coin a phrase, a rounded square. I liked it very much, and there was no question but that this was IT!. As we turned to go away, I saw a face I knew quite well. Who was he?!

Do you ever have those moments when you wish the ground would swallow you up? Normally this man would have been in Saudi Arabia, and in Saudi Arabian dress. He was in neither; he was the most unlikely person to meet in a Geneva jewelers I could think of; maybe he felt the same about me! He was no other than the Deputy Finance Minister of Saudi Arabia, a not inconsequential fellow with whom I had had a lot of dealings over a few year period. One occasion sticks in my mind concerning this man. Saudi Arabia and the US had a joint solar energy program with a funding of one hundred million dollars over those five years. Each year both countries had to put Ten Million Dollars into the "kitty" on October 1st for the coming year. I was Chairman of the Joint

Eric H. Willis

Executive Committee, and we were holding a meeting on September 23rd, or thereabouts. He asked me if the United States would be putting its share of ten million into the "kitty" on time. Crossing my fingers under the table, I said "Yes, I don't see why not". I then asked him the same question about Saudi Arabia. In reply, he reached for his hip pocket, pulled out his wallet, extracted a crumpled piece of paper, unfolded it, put it on the table, and presented me with a check for Ten Million Dollars. How could I ever forget this man!! Maybe it was because I don't buy wedding rings everyday, but at that moment in the jewelers, I not only did I forget his name, but introduced him confidently to Helga as someone else! His name was Mohammed al Turki, and I had introduced him as Ali Khatani, who was not even a Saudi – he was a Moroccan ! Later Al Turki was to be President of Riyadh University. His response to my faux pas was most generous; the moment passed, but I had quite a lot of egg on my face! I have a pair of gold cuff links with the Saudi Coat of Arms that he had presented to me on a previous occasion – they serve to remind me of that evening's embarrassment! But at least we had a Wedding Ring.

27. Tying the Knot

At the end of World War Two, there was an air of understandable optimism about planning the future. Empty lots, scars from the Blitz, which littered London were constant reminders of the need for a "Brave New World". A Royal Commission had been appointed, and to their credit they produced a well thought out document called the "Greater London Plan". The idea was to prevent the pre-war urban sprawl of London outwards by having a "greenbelt" around it and new satellite towns established around that belt. It was an imaginative idea, but like all plans the devil is in the details. Several of these towns came into being, and it is a source of great relief that most did not. The Architecture of Post War England, and its equivalent in Germany as well, was conditioned by materials available and the overriding concern of cost. Liberated from pre war uniformity, post war architects embraced another uniformity all of their own. In England the "brave new world" was brought forth in a concrete and brick idiom that ensured mediocrity and a new-brutalist monotony. Imagination was submerged in the rush to build something new.

One casualty of this thinking was an old coaching village on the road from London to Brighton called Crawley. It's designation as a New Town was hailed as a piece of latter day enlightenment, but the results spoke otherwise The town was to have a new center with a pedestrian precinct, which rapidly became obsolete on the arrival of the Mall, the Supermarket, and the two car family. At the center of this brave failure was the Crawley Town Hall. When Helga and I were last there, in early August, we had visited the Registrar of Births, Marriages, and Deaths   (Affectionately known as Hatches, Matches, and Dispatches) at the Town Hall. It is nice to say something nice about a functionary performing her daily tasks – the lady Registrar could not have been more helpful and diligent. But there were limits to her ability to push matters along. Europe is not like Las Vega – -there are no Drive-in Wedding Chapels where getting married is not much different than getting a hamburger at a MacDonald's, and divorce is even easier. Even in England, they take these things seriously.

We had finally received all the requisite papers, and armed with these we paid a second visit to the Registrar in the first days of September. "Thank you very much", she said, "these look just fine, but now they will have to sent up to Somerset House in London for final authorization". "If everything is fine,' said Helga," why do they have to go up to London?". "Ah, dear," said the Registrar, with a sigh of one bearing an obvious truth to those too dim too see, "you have foreign divorces." Helga was just rising from her seat to protest loudly that <u>we</u> were not foreign, when I whispered in her ear " Yes Dear, <u>here</u>, we are!" This new turn of events was going to make the schedule tight, but it was still doable. In the event we gave notice of marriage, and paid the fees. As often is the case the down payment is modest but the lifetime costs are a different story. Our names were to be publicly displayed in Crawley Town Hall for a week or two for anyone to voice objection, and with a green light from London we could then proceed. If I were to be entrusted with the World's most sensitive secrets, I cannot imagine a better spot to hide them than on a Bulletin Board in the dark and dusty recesses of Crawley Town Hall, England.

Mother Win kindly offered to host us a Reception at the Copthorne Hotel, close by in the country. It was a splendid venue, with a very pleasant ambiance in well kept grounds. This was very generous of her, and was gratefully accepted. The Rev Greene and the Church were also reserved for the afternoon of the16[th], and all we could do now was to hope that the squirrels in Somerset House would consent to our marriage on time. The Registrar had done what she could to expedite the process, and we trusted that she had some influence on the matter. Taking a bit of a chance , we phoned Hertha, Monika, and Nigel in the Washington area, and arranged for them to fly into London,Gatwick Airport, only two miles away, on the morning of the 16th . Son Martin would arrive in Paris from Cleveland on the 12th, via London and the three of us would come over together on the 14th. We all were to stay at an establishment called the "Barnwood Hotel", which was rather threadbare in some respects, but could at a pinch be called adequate. We had stayed there a few times, and it had the virtue of being convenient without asking the prices hotels close to airports normally charge. All was now set---Somerset House, please come through for us! There was nothing else for us to do but wait

As a pleasant interlude, and since the sun was shining for once, a leisurely day in the country might serve to relax the tensions which were inevitably growing. Before returning to Paris, I suggested to Helga that we might visit the Bluebell Line in the Sussex countryside. Steam trains are a passion of mine. As a kid, I could never refrain from sticking my head out of the window, contrary to all instructions, and usually get specks of soot in my eye as a result. There is something about a steam engine; it is alive, it breathes, it snorts, it strives, it whistles, and it smells of that sweet fragrance of a mixture of oil, coal, and steam. Fortunately, I am not alone: volunteers have banded together to preserve this rich part of our heritage of the industrial revolution. Railways in their heyday spawned spurs from local junctions to serve isolated localities, often market towns. The Stations, in the center of town were sometimes memorable structures, and meeting a train was an event. As these spurs became increasingly uneconomic with competition from road transport, they were closed down in large part. But fortunately some have survived due to the determined efforts of some dedicated enthusiasts. They constitute a form of industrial age archaeology. One such preserved line is the Bluebell Line, which runs some beautifully restored engines and rolling stock saved from the scrapheap. These engines were once the Kings of the Iron Road, and in their freshly painted livery, they look and act their part. The Bluebell line runs from Sheffield Park to Horsted Keynes, and runs through some of the most lovely parts of the classic English countryside. If you are ever in that part of the world, I would certainly suggest a detour.

We returned to Paris to wait it out, and of course to tend to the work which never seems to want to wait. Helga got herself a really fine dress for the wedding. I admired it with genuine enthusiasm – it was truly elegant. She then revealed that she had got it at her favorite store, the second-hand boutique in *Rue Civry*. Actually, she was pretty mad because there was one price on it, she bought it at two hundred francs less, only to find when she got home that there was a tag on for two hundred francs less than that, Helga does not take kindly to being diddled, particularly over her own Wedding Dress! A bargain that could have been a better one is not that much of a bargain! She found from the Bank that she couldn't stop the check in France, so played steam with the rather snooty stone faced woman in the store. After threatening to get them blacklisted with the US Embassy, an imaginative but I suspect unrealistic gesture, the woman in desperation gave her a coupon for one hundred francs. Honor was only to some extent satisfied, but she did have a great dress!

To complicate matters, we had a self invited house guest at the end of the week. This which would have been pleasant enough in ordinary circumstances but the timing at that moment was not the best. I think Helga had all of ten minutes to change the bed for Martin's arrival before we dashed off to get our guest to the Departures at Charles de Gaulle Airport only to wait around for Martin to appear at Arrivals. It was great to see him, and I think it was one of the most happy few days I ever spent with him. I ought to say at this point that we later lost Martin in 1994, and so happy memories of this sort are particularly precious. After giving him some sleep, we went out in the evening around the classic sites of Paris ending in Montmartre. We dined at a small restaurant near the Butte, *La Belle Gabrielle* on *Rue Norvins*, with a piano player and a brassy male singer belting out ballads from the Edith Piaff era. It was a bit touristy, naturally, but we loved it and even requested some numbers. The open area on the Butte is usually full of artists offering their wares to eager tourists; it is always fascinating to see someone sitting before an artist, and then see what his rendering of the subject looks like. Sometimes the resemblance is superficial! As it was Martin's Birthday coming up on the 15th, Helga got one of them to do a caricature of him, which fortunately turned out to be a good one.

On the Sunday, Martin went to the Eiffel Tower to look around, and ran into one mighty thunderstorm. He took some pictures of a rainbow enveloping Paris which has to be one of the finest I have ever seen. I took him out to Versailles, and it turned out to be one of those rare occasions when the fountains were on full display. While he was there only a short time, he managed to get some impressions that few visitors get.

On the Sunday evening we packed and were off on a circuitous route by car to Crawley early on Monday. I had to make a call in Brussels at the European Commission, so the first leg of the journey was the rather tedious drive to the Belgian Capital. Helga and Martin caught a cab from the Commission, and "did" Brussels. I find Brussels rather a drab city in many ways, but the main square, *La Grande Place*, almost makes up for it by itself. The sixteenth and seventeenth century architecture surrounds the four sides of the square, and is totally unspoiled. The highlight of their visit was a fine seafood lunch. Martin had a large pot of very fresh *moules,* and he was in seventh heaven. They then grabbed a cab to meet up with me at the EU again around three.

It took about three hours to reach Calais, and had just about time to catch our reservation on the Ferry to England. The "ferry" we were on was in fact a Hovercraft. It rides on a cushion of air at about sixty miles an hour provided the waves are sufficiently cooperative to allow the thing to operate. Fortune was on our side this day, and it was working. We found it a bit of a sporty ride, which is acceptable if you have no need to avail yourself of the "Loo". Helga reported that that was even more sporty!. In just about thirty minutes we arrived in Folkestone. Today, I am sure the Channel Tunnel has robbed people of the thrills of crossing the sea at an altitude of five feet. It was naturally drizzling in England, and after a fish and chip pub dinner, we got to Mother's house by ten. It had been a hard and tiring way to get the two hundred miles in a direct line from Paris.

I had an appointment at the British Department of Energy in London on the Tuesday, and went up to Victoria Station by train. They were always having new bosses, and I seemed to get roped in by my friends to put in a good word for their programs with the "new boy". This particular fellow had got a bee in his bonnet about the subject of fusion energy; he wanted to cancel the budget item immediately. Yet Britain was the host to one of the three large Tokomak Controlled Fusion Machines in the world , "JET" standing for the Joint European Torus. The Country thus had rather a large stake in the Program. The new"Boss Man', whose name I have mercifully long forgotten, was a thorough agnostic and if it had been possible to demolish JET with a sledge hammer he would have gladly swung the first blow. He was a political ideologue of the right wing of the Conservative Party, and although he was personally pleasant to me, he engaged in an endless anti fusion energy soliloquy. If there had been a scintilla of logic hidden somewhere, I and everyone else in the room certainly missed it. I remember standing outside on the Thames Embankment, waiting to hail a cab, thinking how it was possible to achieve cohesion in joint international projects when the principal political actors changed so rapidly, and with ideas ranging from one extreme to another. And all this on the day before my Wedding! There must be better ways to earn a living.

We were up early on Wednesday the 16th to meet the 8.00am plane from Washington at Gatwick. Unfortunately, it must have been blown by hurricane force winds over the Atlantic and arrived an hour and a half early. Three tired and forlorn individuals, thinking they had either been forgotten or arrived at the wrong airport, were ready to be transported to the hotel for some well needed sleep. Having deposited our Trans Atlantic guests in their respective beds, Helga and I did the last minute arrangements at the Copthorne for the reception – the room was very well appointed, with a large oval table to seat about twenty guests. Hertha had invited George Vine, an old friend of hers who lived in Kent, and I had invited two old school friends and their wives, Eric and Mary Boobyer and Don and Catherine Anniss. Don was the Doctor who got innocently involved in the "cocaine" affair. (see Chapter 19). My sister Doreen and her family made up the rest of the Guest List. The next appointment was at the Church to ensure that all was in order there. Much to our relief, all the paper work had arrived, and the Reverend had at last got final permission to marry us. We needed a quick afternoon snooze lest we show our fatigue!

The Ceremony was at five o'clock. It was a bright Fall afternoon, which in England means on the cool side. I was fearful that Helga's lovely silk dress might need a layer of winter woollies underneath. I cannot think of a nicer marriage ceremony, and it is a memory that Helga and I will certainly cherish. Our three children duly signed the register as witnesses, thus making them guarantors of the newly weds. The reception was everything we could have wished for, with an excellent menu of Consommé, Coquilles St Jacques, Rack of Lamb, and a Flambé dessert. The wine was of excellent quality, and flowed freely. Cigars were smoked by some with whom one would not associate such an indulgence! It was some very tired but very happy folk who went back to the hotel that night.

Nigel, Martin and Monika went to Brighton the following day, while Hertha returned with her cousin-by-marriage, George Vine, to his home in Hastings, Kent.

Maybe it is a testament to our state of near total exhaustion at that point, but I have absolutely no recollection of what Helga and I did that day!. The youngsters were out on the town at some night club later that evening, although it would be interesting to know what passes as a "hot spot" in that part of the world. They seem to have had a competition as to who could consume the hottest curry, which makes for frightening images of their digestive systems that night.

Having recovered a little by the following day, we ventured up to London on the Friday, with Nigel going by train to his maternal grandparents for the day. We , Monika, Martin, Helga and I, managed to pack a lot in to a short time, having lunch at the "Punch and Judy" pub in Covent Garden; a taxi ride to St Paul's Cathedral; a visit to the Tower of London with the obligatory photograph with a "Beefeater"; and a boat ride up the Thames to Westminster. A day full of wonderful memories for Helga and the kids. As for me, I had spent three years at King's College, London during the War, and so it was an old stomping ground. It was quite a thrill to share it with my "new" Family. Martin, who would go nowhere without a car, drove off to his grandmother's as Nigel was coming back by train. It was a fitting end to an adventurous week away for people of any age.

Saturday saw the American contingent on their way back to Washington and Cleveland respectively. After giving my Mother a big hug and a heartfelt "thank you", Helga and I headed for the Channel Port of Newhaven for the four hour crossing to Dieppe. The drive back to Paris was somewhat anticlimactic, rain and drizzle all the way. We arrived "home" tired but very happy, and we opened a bottle of Henkel Tocken as a celebration at dinner. Alone, Home, and Married at last – we had striven hard for this very moment, and here it had finally arrived. I misjudged the power of Henkel Trocke – -the cork flew out with a loud "pop" – and opened my forehead right between the eyes. Blood spurted all over the place. What a let down – but there was nothing else to do but roar with laughter.

At a senior Staff Meeting at the IEA the next day, Wally Hopkins took one look at the gash on my head, and exclaimed " Whatever happened to you?!"

Ulf Lantzke sat back, inhaled on his cheroot, slowly puffed out some blue smoke, spread out his expressive hands, and with a broad smile said,

"Why, he just got married!!"